Wellspring *of* Compassion

Wellspring _of_ Compassion

Self-Care for Sensitive People Healing from Trauma

Sonia Connolly

Sundown Healing Arts
Portland, Oregon

Published by Sundown Healing Arts, Portland, Oregon
SundownHealingArts.com
Requests for permission to make copies of any part of the work can be submitted to permissions@sundownhealingarts.com.
For bulk orders, write to orders@sundownhealingarts.com.

File under: SELF-HELP/ABUSE

Printed in the United States of America
Cover design: Beth Olson
Lotus graphics: Arlin Robins

Library of Congress Control Number: 2011938558
ISBN-13: 978-0-9839038-0-2
FIRST EDITION

This publication is not intended as a substitute for the advice of health care professionals. Internet addresses were accessible at the time this book went to press. Content of referenced websites is solely that of their sponsors and does not necessarily reflect the opinions of the author of this book.

I give thanks for help unknown already on the way.

This book is dedicated to those who need help right now.
May you find what you seek in these pages.

Acknowledgments

My thanks to Patricia Nan Anderson for practical guidance and encouragement that helped bring this book into being. My thanks to Kyra Plume for the detailed critique with the little hearts at the parts you liked. Thanks to Jennifer Casteen and Marisa Wood for useful feedback on the first draft. Thanks to Carrie Mook Bridgman for copyediting and support. Your help made this a better book.

My thanks to each client who courageously shared your process with me in session. Thanks to each person who responded to my newsletter to tell me how an article touched you.

My thanks to all those who have gone before, offering a book or a website or a kind word to guide my growth.

Contents

Introduction: Welcome_____1

    Signs of Trauma_____5

    Signs of Sensitivity_____7

1: Find Support_____9

    Deepen Your Roots, Spread Your Branches_____11

    First-Aid for Desperate Moments_____14

    Disclose Pain, Find Support_____17

    A Boundary-Nourishing Healer Search_____20

    100 Percent On Your Own Side_____25

    Add Peace to Your Life_____28

    Resources_____30

2: Celebrate Your Survival Tools_____31

    The Gift of Resistance_____32

    Tell a Story About Denial_____34

    Gain Awareness of Dissociation_____38

    Addiction as Emotion Management_____41

    Behind the Curtain of Obsessive Thoughts_____45

    Calm Your Inner Critic_____48

    Resources_____52

3: Connect with Your Self_____55

    Meditation: Safe Space for Noticing_____56

    Many Voices, All Valid_____60

    Befriend Your Pain_____63

    Invite Your Longing to Tea_____67

    Needs Amnesty Day_____70

Sensitivities: Your Self-Care Guide_____73
Resources_____76

4: Recognize Abuse_____**77**
Demand Respect, Not Victim-Blaming_____78
"Trust Me!" and Other Red Flags_____81
Step Away from Double Binds_____85
Emotional Abuse: You Deserve Better_____89
Grieve Neglectful Mothering_____92
Spiritual Abuse: Take Back Your Faith_____96
Resources_____99

5: Understand Post-Traumatic Stress Disorder (PTSD)_**101**
Ups and Downs of Healing from Trauma_____103
Remember at Your Own Pace_____107
Flashbacks: Experience Distress in Safety_____111
Anxiety, Your Relaxation Coach_____115
Frozen! Thaw from Surrender_____119
Accept Suicidal Feelings_____123
Resources_____127

6: Heal Your Boundaries_____**129**
Say Yes to Your Boundaries_____131
Claim Your Space, Breathe into Your Back_____134
Who Owns That Anger?_____137
Just-Right Visibility_____140
Inner Child Lost -n- Found_____143
Haunted by Shame? Change Your Committee_____146
Resources_____150

7: Learn to Thrive_____**151**
Create: Walk into Fog_____152

Choose Your Traditions_____156

The Joy of Maintenance_____159

Compassion for the Drama Triangle_____162

Not Again! Tame Your Fiercest Patterns_____165

Allow Self-Forgiveness_____168

Resources_____172

Afterword: Wellspring of Compassion_____173

Glossary_____175

About the Author_____179

Introduction: Welcome

Welcome to support and comfort whether you are new to healing or an old hand, whether the trauma is long past or ongoing.

Your experience is valid. Trauma survivors and sensitive people are both considered Other by mainstream culture. Flooded by that viewpoint, we often treat our own experience as a problem to be solved. This book accepts your experience as valid and important.

Explore self-care. Self-care can sound like an obligation, one more item on a long to-do list. Self-care can sound like abandonment if we were emotionally or physically neglected as children and still long for someone to rescue us. Self-care can sound selfish, self-indulgent, or forbidden when we are accustomed to caring for others first.

Caring for and about yourself includes resting from self-improvement, reaching out for help, and expressing clear boundaries. True self-care is self-compassion, allowing yourself to be exactly who you are right now. Grounded in self-compassion, you will be able to offer assistance to others and help them learn self-compassion as well.

Still growing. I started my own healing process full of

impatient enthusiasm. I was sure that if I worked hard enough and figured out the right choices, I would be healed in no time. Twenty years later, many aspects of my life have improved and I still encounter challenges as well.

Nowadays, fewer stones block my access to the wellspring of compassion within me, and I feel a seeping certainty that I am already good enough. I understand now that compassion was always there waiting while I hunted for it everywhere except inside myself.

Turn within. It takes a leap of faith to stop looking for external permission and trust the compassionate voice welling up inside. Internal critical voices are loudly emphatic, and they are often supported by external voices as well.

These articles were written over a three year period for my monthly newsletter.* Each one focuses on an aspect of healing from trauma by reconnecting with your body, your emotions, and your felt experience. The material is gathered from reading others' wise words, from listening to my body, and from working with my clients.

Take your time. Lotus plants take root underwater and grow toward the surface where the flowers open to light and air. At the beginning of each article, a lotus flower invites you to pause, breathe, and open to your self.

You can read this book as a continuous whole or dip in and out, focusing on the topics that are most alive for you right now. The examples are intentionally mild to avoid additional triggering. If you feel anxious, impatient, or bored, you can take a break or skip the parts that are difficult for you.

---

* Read new articles and subscribe to my free monthly newsletter: www.TraumaHealed.com/articles/

As you read, listen to your body and notice what is true for you with gentle awareness. You can try the suggested exercises and experiments when you have an uninterrupted block of time to yourself, or they can be done in bits and pieces as you go about your day, whenever you have time to think and feel.

Resolving trauma held in the body is an ongoing process. As you tune in to your body and your inner self with the suggestions in this book, you may connect with upsetting information about past trauma. Especially at the beginning, it is important to proceed gently and with support.

Overview. The articles are grouped into seven themes.

1. **Find Support.** Support and trust are complex issues for trauma survivors. Reach for both external and internal support and meet your Inner Nurturer.

2. **Celebrate Your Survival Tools.** Learn to meet yourself where you are now. Rather than devalue the tools and behaviors that helped you survive, celebrate them and yourself. Negotiate a truce with your Inner Critic.

3. **Connect with Your Self.** Trauma often catapults us out of our bodies. Bring kind attention to your emotions and sensations to reconnect with your self.

4. **Recognize Abuse.** Trauma can be shockingly sudden and obvious, or it can be subtle, ongoing, and difficult to name. Be your own ally in response to victim-blaming, double binds, neglect, and other types of covert abuse.

5. **Understand Post-Traumatic Stress Disorder (PTSD).** PTSD is a label for your nervous system's long-term response to trauma. Learn about compassionate approaches to the symptoms and how to

find healing.

6. **Heal Your Boundaries.** Most trauma damages physical and emotional boundaries. Reconnect with and express your preferences to help your boundaries heal. When "They" disapprove of your decisions, hire a new internal committee.

7. **Learn to Thrive.** It is not just about healing the past. Explore tools for shaping the life you want and finding joy in the present.

Check the **Glossary** for definitions when you encounter unfamiliar terms.

Trust your Self. With validation and support, your self-trust will heal. As you shift from fear to curiosity, you will find new ways to be kind to yourself and remove the stones that block your wellspring of compassion.

Signs of Trauma

Trauma is defined as an event or ongoing situation that overwhelms your resources to handle it. During traumatic events, memories are stored as direct sensory information rather than processed into a story. Physical and emotional shocks are also stored in the body.

The body and spirit do their best to work around the unprocessed memories and shock, but there is a continuing toll on energy, emotional well-being, and physical health. Over time, signs of unprocessed trauma urge you to seek healing.

Signs of trauma include:

- Chronic pain or recurring injuries which respond to treatment slowly or not at all
- Constant tension, inability to relax
- Difficulty with basic self-care (laundry, meals, showers)
- Consistently shallow breathing
- Chaotic, painful relationships
- A fiercely critical internal voice that will not quit
- Strong startle response to unexpected touch, sound, or light
- Frequent anxiety, panic, or terror
- Frequent numbness or blankness
- Suicidal thoughts or feelings
- Avoidance of emotions through alcohol, other

drugs, sugar, exercise, overwork, etc.
- A feeling of impending doom even when life is going well
- Dissociation - consistent spaciness, a feeling of distance from current experience
- Flashbacks – a re-experiencing of a past event through one or more senses (hearing, sight, emotions, etc.)

People experience a full range of conscious memory after trauma, from complete details to complete amnesia. If you have some of these signs, but do not remember any trauma, trust your inner wisdom as the final authority about your experiences.

Signs of Sensitivity

Do you wince or leave the room when the music is loud? Do you absorb anger or joy from people around you? Are you the first to notice when someone is having a hard day? Do you get overwhelmed easily and need time and quiet to recover? Do you need to be careful of what you eat, drink, and breathe to feel healthy?

Innate sensitivity varies. In her book *The Highly Sensitive Person,**** Elaine Aron describes the characteristics and challenges of sensitive people. In her research, she found that sensitivity is an innate characteristic. About 20% of babies are born sensitive.

Many characteristics of sensitive people overlap with signs of trauma, since trauma can overwhelm the nervous system and leave it more reactive than before. A sensitive person who experiences trauma faces a double challenge.

It is easy to think of someone who blasts his music as inconsiderate, but a less sensitive person may not even notice the music volume. Similarly, some people react to trauma by shutting down and becoming less reactive, not more.

A comfortable environment. Whether sensitivity is innate, trauma-related, or both, it is important to provide ourselves with an environment that is calm enough to be comfortable. Feeling constantly overwhelmed stresses the whole body and leads to escalating physical symptoms.

---

* Elaine Aron, *The Highly Sensitive Person*, Broadway Books, 1996. Sensitivity self-test: www.hsperson.com/pages/test.htm

Sometimes we remain unaware of physical sensitivities until we are struggling with the symptoms they cause. Constant fatigue and intestinal distress led me to discover that I cannot tolerate wheat gluten. Chronic joint pain and headaches led me to avoid fragrances and chemicals as well.

I believe both sensitivities arise from a nervous system overburdened by past trauma. As I provide myself with an environment free of the foods and chemicals that cause me stress, as well as avoiding other forms of stress, my nervous system can heal. Over time, my nervous system becomes more resilient and does not react as strongly to my environment.

As I learn what my system needs to be comfortable, I notice a decrease in other symptoms as well, both emotional and physical. Accidentally eating gluten leads to a resurgence of anxiety, despair, inability to focus, losing words, confusion, repeated yawning, facial acne, physical inertia, extreme flatulence, aversion to drinking water, and disconnection from appetite and hunger signals.

The emotional symptoms surprised me until I remembered that the gut has many neurochemical receptors, its own complex nervous system, and a direct connection to the brain via the vagus nerve. While the physical symptoms are uncomfortable, the brain fog and despair motivate me to scrupulously avoid gluten. Feeling productive and resilient is ample reward for limiting my food choices.

The following pages offer ways to find support, calm your nervous system, and heal from the after-effects of trauma. As you listen inward with compassion, you will discover what you want in your life and how to move toward it.

1: Find Support

Self-care includes defining your goals in a compassionate way, having first-aid available for desperate moments, reaching out to others for support, finding support within, and adding peace to your life wherever you can.

Tara Miller, MEd., self-proclaimed spiritual seeker/healer, describes her process:*

"I think it is important to get as clear a picture as you can about what you want peace to look like in your life (think about it, write about it, bead about it, collage); then while living your daily life you need to simultaneously keep attuned to opportunities that will lead you there, and make those choices (as risky as they may seem). It is in those choices that progress is actually made.

"So many times we choose to stay the same because we are comfortable with our trauma. We can even wrap ourselves in it with the idea that we are working on it; then get frustrated with the progress we have made.

"Alternatively, we can make a new blanket with the

---

* Tara Miller, personal communication, 2010.

fabric of our vision for a peaceful life, wrap ourselves in it, and work on it. I make no self-righteous claim that I have accomplished peace in my life as an end, but just like meditation gives you an image to come back to when your mind wanders on a thought, I need that peaceful vision to wrap myself in when I see myself holding on to the old fabric."

Do you have an image or metaphor that supports your healing process? As you read this section, notice opportunities for a supportive image to develop within you. Do you feel inspired to make art about your image?

Deepen Your Roots, Spread Your Branches

The metaphor of healing as a journey permeates our language. "One step at a time." "Find your path." "I'll get there someday." The assumptions hidden in this metaphor invite painful comparisons and judgments, including:

- We want to travel from unsatisfactory Here to much improved There.
- Progress is visible and directed.
- Moving slowly makes the journey take longer.
- The only successful outcome is reaching There and ending the journey.

Instead of travel, I prefer to think of healing from trauma as growth, like a tree becoming taller and wider and more intricately itself every year. Whether awkwardly pruned, attacked by insects, or struck by lightning, trees start where they are and continue growing.

Deepen your roots by exploring yourself and your past. You are not limited to one physical place like a tree, but you do have only one history. You can reach your roots into different parts of it and change how you perceive your history over time, finding pockets of nourishing compost in both your own and your ancestors' stories.

Your physical body forms part of your root system, guiding, supporting, and constraining you as you grow. Get to know your innate strengths and talents, as well as your weaknesses and limitations.

Explore with kindness. Your body, your experiences, and your responses are unique. You deserve acceptance for all of yourself, including the parts judged for being disabled or abnormal or deficient or too much.

Acceptance is not always calm. Allow yourself to mourn your losses, rage at injustice and abuse, and celebrate your successes. Stand with yourself as a kind witness to your experiences.

Find your strengths. As you connect with your roots, you may find it easier to list weaknesses than strengths. Make a list of weaknesses, and then beside each one note how you compensate for that weakness. These compensations are some of your strengths and capabilities.

Sometimes we assume that what is easy for us is easy for everyone, or that strengths require struggle. What actions are easy for you? They can be in the physical realm, like swimming long distances, or the emotional realm, like connecting with young children, or the mental realm, like memorizing poetry. These are strengths as well.

Stretch your branches. Like a securely rooted tree growing toward the sunlight, stretch your branches by following your internal impulses toward what delights you and feeds you.

Do you have goals for your healing process? Make a list. Beside each goal, note how you want to feel when you accomplish it. Those feelings are your wider goals.

Are there any ways you already have those feelings in your current life? Keep your desired feelings in mind over the next few days, and notice if you have any glimpses of them. As you make large or small decisions, choose based on how you predict you will feel. Celebrate as you grow toward your goals.

Barriers to growth. Sometimes physical barriers and missing resources impede a tree's growth. When you reach for delight, do you encounter resistance? Are you getting the water and light and nutrients you need to support your growth?

Sometimes the goals themselves form a barrier when they are based on other people's expectations and definitions of success. Is there a double bind making every choice look wrong?

Notice the barriers you encounter and, like a persistent tree, grow around and through them. This can take a long time. Give yourself permission not to know yet how it will happen. There is no rush.

When you feel blocked, then, like a tree in winter, rest and wait. Keep your goals in the background as you pay attention to the present and make tiny incremental changes when you can. Someday a breakthrough will surprise you.

Grow into your unique shape. As you grow and heal and reach new heights, your perspective will change on your goals and possibilities. Where some of your goals included fitting in with others, you may realize that "normal" is an illusion and you are growing into a shape defined by your own history and desires. As you stretch and change, you may need to grieve relationships that no longer fit.

Life does not begin after you heal. This is already your life, happening right now. Growth and change and healing continue as long as you are alive, in your own time and your own rhythm.

First-Aid for Desperate Moments

Your healing goals probably include feeling better more often and knowing what to do when you feel terrible. You may already have a handy list of friends, family, or professionals to call in a crisis and another list of music to play and soothing actions to take.

Sometimes you are on your own, or have already tried everything you can think of. The following phrases provide first-aid assistance when you need to feel better *right now*. They are collected here for quick reference.

"I give thanks for help unknown already on the way."* When you feel alone and trapped and cannot imagine how the situation could improve, this phrase brings hope. Maybe a change is quietly building underground, or you will encounter someone tomorrow who will mention just the idea you are looking for.

Your desperate younger selves will appreciate knowing that things already got better, and your desperate current self will breathe a little easier with the possibility that a shift is on the way.

"It ended." It is healing to express old pent-up emotions. It is also healing to interrupt them with knowledge that they are old, and the traumatic events that caused them did end. Carry this phrase with you into flashbacks and let it anchor you in the present. (See page 121.)

---

* Author unknown.

"This problem is already solved." After a contentious conversation or a fruitless search, this phrase helps you take a step back and drop the struggle. Perhaps your conversational opponent did hear your boundary and will not repeat the offensive behavior.

Perhaps you already own an object that fits your need. This worked for me after a frustrating search for supportive walking shoes. Aha, I can wear my hiking boots, even though they are not officially meant for urban walking.

"I am doing the right thing." When you are caught in a spiral of self-criticism and shame, this phrase shifts your attention to all the things you are doing right. (See page 50.)

"What if this isn't mine?" When you are experiencing an intense emotion such as anger, anxiety, despair, or attraction and nothing you do changes it, ask yourself this question. Sensitive people are prone to picking up emotions from others. If the emotion does belong to someone else, you will feel immediate relief. (See page 139.)

"Don't go to the hardware store for milk,"* and **"Not a good match."** If your needs are not met by individuals or businesses, it is tempting to blame yourself or treat them as enemies. When you acknowledge that your needs are valid but this is not a good match, it gives you the freedom to peacefully disengage and look elsewhere. (See page 26.)

"Don't compare your insides to someone else's outsides."* We constantly judge ourselves in comparison to others. Their lives seem smooth and effortless compared to our ragged struggles. When we remember that their struggles and situations are invisible to us, we can be kinder to ourselves. (See page 152.)

---

* Author unknown.

"I am already good enough." When you receive stinging criticism from yourself or someone else, this phrase helps you regain perspective. With an external message, also try reversing "I" and "you" to see if the criticism is more true about the speaker.

"I don't need fixing." When you seek support, remember that at the core there is nothing wrong with you. Move toward support that invites you to feel more whole rather than more broken. (See page 79.)

"It's okay to be where I am right now," and **"I am having the experience of..."** Yes, it is uncomfortable to be desperate and in pain. It is also okay to be here until it shifts. It will shift, eventually. Meanwhile, breathe, notice your experience, and wait it out. (See page 165.)

Do you have phrases that reliably help you? Make signs and post them where you will see them in the midst of desperation.

Disclose Pain, Find Support

A desperate moment may motivate you to look for external support, but it can take time and planning to find it. After a traumatic event, many survivors experience the secondary trauma of isolation and lack of support.

Overwhelming events are difficult to put into words, and the effects last longer than most people expect. Survivors may need to tell their story repeatedly, or they may not want to discuss it at all, and yet long for contact and support. It is deeply nourishing to share painful thoughts and feelings with a receptive listener.

Finding a receptive listener can be difficult for many reasons. People may be too busy, or uncomfortable with "negative" emotions, or overwhelmed with their own needs for support. They may turn away, change the subject, tell the survivor to "cheer up", give advice, or chime in with their own story.

An unhelpful response can feel like a personal failure to a struggling survivor even though, ironically, would-be supporters are responding to their own needs and not to the survivor at all.

When you gain clarity on what you are looking for and allow plenty of time for your disclosure, you increase the chances of getting exactly what you want.

1. Honor your needs. The first step to finding nourishing support is to gently inquire into what you need. Imagine the response you want in elaborate detail. You might want your supporter to stay quiet, ask questions, or give reassurance. You might want a touch on your shoulder, a hug, or a room's worth of space.

What specific words and actions mean "support" to you? In past conversations, which responses caused you to tense up or turn away, and which caused you to relax or sigh with relief?

As you pay attention to your need for support, gently notice any feelings that arise. Some people have "shoulds" around keeping silent, toughing it out alone, or not admitting weakness. There may also be shame around the pain being disclosed, grief from past attempts to reach for support, or longing for someone who is no longer available. What comes up for you?

2. Honor your pain. How do you respond to your pain? Even as you long for support, your Inner Critic may echo harsh responses you received as a child. Do you hear an affirming inner voice as well? Supportive responses received from the outside help build your Inner Nurturer.

3. Choose a supporter. As you think about different people in your life or consider disclosing to someone new to you, the sensitive barometer of your body will help you make choices. Pay attention to the same physical responses you noticed as you were honoring your needs: tensing or relaxing, holding your breath or breathing deeply, looking down or looking outward, shutting down or opening up.

4. Disclose in steps. Whether you speak with a professional or a friend, gradually increase the level of disclosure, possibly in separate conversations, and proceed only if you are comfortable with the responses you receive:

- Broach the topic of painful feelings in general.
- Ask if the person is comfortable providing

emotional support.

- Share your strengths and the ways you are taking care of yourself.
- Clearly state the responses and support you are hoping for.
- Disclose a piece of your painful thoughts and feelings.
- Check in about how you both feel after the conversation.

Continue to reach out until you receive the support you seek. You may need rest between attempts. Notice how your body responds during both positive and negative experiences. Each attempt will help you attune to your physical responses around risk, trust and support.

Support for others. As you learn about reaching for the support you need, apply similar steps when you are asked to give support to others. Tune in to your body to notice whether you want to give support to that person in that moment. If not, politely state that it is not a good time. If you do want to give support, ask what sort of responses the person is looking for, and give your full attention during the conversation.

Afterward, check in with your emotions and physical sensations again. Supportive conversations can be positive for everyone involved.

Build connections. Disclosing painful feelings can feel risky and vulnerable, and at the same time, receiving support is powerfully nurturing and life-affirming. You can reduce the risks by going slowly and checking in with yourself at each step. Strengthened connections with yourself and others will be your reward.

A Boundary-Nourishing Healer Search

Many people seek professional support while healing from trauma. It can be unexpectedly difficult to find a healer who is a good match while already struggling with issues of safety, trust, and boundaries.

There are healers for the mind, the body, and the spirit. This article focuses on healing bodywork such as massage, Reiki, or various other modalities. Caring touch from a trusted practitioner can help you calm anxiety, reconnect with your body, and gradually release frozen trauma memories.

Bodywork can also be a trigger for anxiety, memories, and boundary issues. The search for healers and building trust with them can be both challenging and healing.

The following process helps you clarify your boundaries and conduct your search gradually. The process can be generalized to find a psychotherapist, construction contractor, job, or even romantic partner. The steps can be done out of order, a little bit here and there, in whatever way suits you best.

Optionally, get a notebook to collect your observations. The steps are: describe your NOs, describe your YESes, gather names of practitioners, interview by phone, and schedule a session.

1. Describe your NOs. You may be shaking your head and saying, "I would NEVER…"

- "…allow a stranger to touch me."

- "...take off my clothes."
- "...receive bodywork from a woman."

That's great! Make a list of your boundaries, and promise yourself to honor them. Throughout your search, assume that you can receive what you need in a way that feels safe to you. Some bodywork practitioners will meet with you first or do energy work without touching you until you feel comfortable. Many kinds of bodywork are done over clothes. Men offer bodywork too. Check in with your body and notice how it feels to have these strong boundaries in place.

Your NOs and YESes may change over time. You may wish they were different now or feel external pressure to ignore them. Paradoxically, there is more room for change when you honor your current boundaries without forcing or expecting them to change.

2. Describe your YESes. Now write a paragraph or list describing what you do want. In a perfect world, what would this healer be like?

Some ideas to start with:

- Respectful of boundaries
- Open to feedback
- Knowledgeable about PTSD and trauma
- Kind, compassionate
- Intuitive
- Comfortable location, fee

3. Gather names of practitioners. This is where a notebook comes in handy to keep track of names, phone numbers, and responses. Scraps of paper, backs of envelopes, and notes in the corner of planner pages all work, too.

Ask for recommendations based on your YESes and NOs

from people whose judgment you trust. You may be comfortable revealing that you have PTSD, or you can ask "for a friend," or perhaps you will decide that you are only ready to speak to a few people. Professionals such as psychotherapists, doctors, and other bodywork practitioners can be good resources.

Search the web with keywords (for example *bodywork PTSD your-city your-state*) and in practitioner directories for specific types of bodywork. Some gentle, awareness-based modalities are CranioSacral Therapy, Feldenkrais Method, Reiki, Rosen Method, and Somatic Experiencing.

4. Interview by phone. The day will come when you are ready to call one or more of the healers on your list. You might get voicemail, a receptionist, or, sometimes, the practitioner will answer the phone in person. You may also be able to make initial contact by email.

If you leave a message, all you need to say is that you are gathering information to make an appointment, and leave your phone number. Twice. It is challenging enough to wait for a call back without wondering if they can reach you.

When you do reach the practitioner, it is helpful to have a list of questions that cover your YESes and NOs. Also pay attention to the reactions in your body. Do you relax or become more tense during the conversation? It is okay to be nervous – notice how the practitioner handles that.

Sample questions:

- "What's your experience with doing bodywork for PTSD?"
- "How does your work help with... (general symptom)?"
- "How soon can I expect results?"

- "I need… (name a YES or a NO). How do you handle that?"
- "What do you charge?"
- "What's your cancellation policy?" (Useful to know, and tells you about boundaries.)
- "Is there anything else I should know about working with you?"

Note that you do not need to tell details of your trauma or symptoms over the phone, especially if that is hard for you.

During the conversation, you may reach a clear positive or negative decision about making an appointment, or you may end the conversation by saying you need to think about it. Ideally, the healer will support you in trusting your judgment.

5. Schedule a session. You decided to schedule a body-work session. Again, it is okay to be nervous. Breathe, stay grounded, and keep noticing how your body is feeling.

Remember that you can change your mind at any point before or during the session. You may still need to pay, depending on the cancellation policy. Perhaps honoring your need to leave or cancel is exactly the therapy you needed that day.

During the session, as much as you can, share your needs with the healer, especially if you feel pain or distress. Some discomfort may be part of your process, but it does not help to become overwhelmed the way you were in the original trauma. Ask any questions that come up for you. You can expect a healer to actively help you listen to your truth at every step.

Trust will build over time. Do not force yourself to trust. If the healer is a good fit, you will melt into the safety with a huge sense of relief.

A healer may be helpful to you for one, a few, or many sessions. Check in with your body about rescheduling just as you did for the first appointment. A long-term bodywork practitioner can be a refuge, supporter, and teacher as you move through the PTSD recovery process.

Celebrate each step you take toward finding a healer, each session you schedule, each change you notice. Some changes will be obvious: less physical or emotional pain, new tools to handle anxiety, more flexibility. Some may be more subtle: more ease in speaking your truth, clearer boundaries, deeper breathing.

Best wishes for your search!

100 Percent On Your Own Side

"A moment of self-compassion can change your entire day. A string of such moments can change the course of your life." — Christopher Germer*

Support from others helps you develop a kind, supportive internal voice.

My Inner Nurturer knows I always deserve respect and love. She helps me trust my perceptions rather than taking a vote from the people around me. She replaces "should" with "could" every time I hear it or say it to myself. She is deeply, unhesitatingly compassionate about my pain.

My Inner Critic (page 48) has a lot to say on the subject of Inner Nurturers. "Silly. Self-indulgent. Dangerous. What will other people think?" My shoulders hunch defensively toward my ears.

Calm at the core. My Inner Nurturer helps me breathe through my defensive reaction and observe the criticism without letting it knock me off course. When I connect with being 100% on my own side, I feel settled and calm at my core, even during emotional storms.

Your Inner Nurturer may have a different name. Robyn Posin calls hers Mommy Inside**. In her book *The Obsidian*

---

* Christopher Germer, *The Mindful Path to Self-Compassion*, Guilford Press, 2009.

** Robyn Posin, "Love Yourself."
www.forthelittleonesinside.com/mpage/lovyrslf.html

ბ 25 ൽ

Mirror, Louise Wisechild calls hers Carrie.* Yours might be your Inner Ally, Inner Healer, or any other name you choose.

A door into sanctuary. Inner Nurturers are solidly convinced that you are doing it right, whatever "it" is. They know that you are doing your absolute best with the resources and information available to you, and if you could do better, you would. When your back is to the wall, they open a door into sanctuary.

Your Inner Nurturer contains your self-trust and confidence about your place in the world. Our right to be here cannot be proven, only assumed, and Inner Nurturers confidently assume it.

Absorb acceptance. Some people's Inner Nurturers develop by internalizing the consistent, loving care they received in childhood. Others received abusive or neglectful parenting and develop an Inner Nurturer later as part of healing. Both as children and as adults, our Inner Nurturers gleefully absorb accepting language whenever we hear it.

A friend told me once, "Don't go to the hardware store for milk." It had not occurred to me before that maybe no one is at fault when there is a mismatch between a situation and my expectations, just as there is nothing wrong with wanting milk, nor with a hardware store for not stocking it. Now my Inner Nurturer reminds me when I forget.

Practice nurturing. In addition to absorbing non-judgmental ideas wherever you find them, develop your Inner Nurturer by practicing on your own.

- Meditation builds the nurturing skills of noticing reactions and accepting what is.

---

* Louise Wisechild, *The Obsidian Mirror*, Seal Press, 2003.

- Supportive voices on your internal committee (page 146) create more room for your Inner Nurturer to emerge.
- Your sensitivities encourage you to honor your preferences.
- When you notice self-doubt, imagine that you support yourself 100%. What would you do differently if you trusted yourself?

Inner Critics worry. If you think that you "should" be more on your own side, and that if you were just more healed this would be easier, and that your own quiet (or loud) Inner Nurturer does not measure up, you are hearing your Inner Critic's voice instead. Inner Critics worry about the power and vulnerability of being 100% on our own side, and do their best to protect us from it with their usual tools.

Notice your responses to your Inner Critic's concerns. Do you shrink away, argue, tense up? Listen for your Inner Nurturer's voice in your responses. What would someone say if they had your back? Your Inner Nurturer is right there in that knowledge of your inner truth.

From self-doubt to self-trust. When a tiny voice inside says, "I want... (something wildly new and different)," or "I don't want... (something you have tolerated for years)," your Inner Nurturer celebrates the information about your boundaries. When your intuition and your feelings react strongly but "unreasonably", your Inner Nurturer knows there is always a good reason.

Being 100% on our own side gives us a solid place to stand when someone tries to sway us with manipulation. Best of all, it interrupts the vicious cycle of self-doubt and self-justification with the sweet relief of self-trust.

Add Peace to Your Life

For a long time I thought my life would become peaceful after I resolved every issue I was facing and achieved every success I desired. After a while, my Inner Nurturer helped me notice that new issues and goals kept arriving without pause, and I needed to make peace a priority now, in the midst of struggle. Making peace a priority has improved my life immensely.

Suggestions for adding peace to your life right now:

- Make a cup of hot tea. Cup your hands around it. Sip it slowly.
- Take a short walk (even if the weather is bad) and notice the buildings, plants, pavement, and earth around you. How does your body feel as you walk?
- Take a bath. Add Epsom salts or your favorite bubble bath.
- Write a thank-you note to someone. Mail it.
- Breathe. Let your ribs expand as you inhale, hold it for a moment, and then let the air flow out of you. Do it again.
- Meditate. Similar to Breathing (above), but do it for 5-20 minutes. When you notice you are distracted, gently bring your attention back to your breath.
- Play your favorite music recording. Sing along as loud as you want.

- Get together with a friend. Tell each other the truth about the struggles and triumphs in your life.
- Find a kind of dancing you enjoy. Do it often.
- Curl up with a favorite book.
- Leave five minutes early for your next destination. Enjoy the journey.
- Exchange hand or foot rubs with a friend. Give each other lots of feedback about what feels good.

Feel free to copy these and post them prominently where they will remind you to take a break when you need one. Add your favorites, too.

I wish you many moments of peaceful relaxation.

Resources

Pema Chodron's *Start Where You Are: A Guide to Compassionate Living*, Shambhala Publications, 2001, is a collection of brief essays about Buddhist slogans which can help you find your way around barriers to light and warmth.

The multi-page web article "How to Choose a Competent Counselor" has good information on selecting support. While much of the article is specific to professional therapy, the page about "Finding the Answer You Already Know" applies to supportive friendships as well.
www.metanoia.org/choose/

The Practitioners page on my website contains a list of recommended practitioners in Portland, Oregon, as well as links to directories of practitioners around the country.
www.traumahealed.com/resources-practitioners.html

Robyn Posin writes about how she developed her Mommy Inside in "Loving Yourself."
www.forthelittleonesinside.com/mpage/lovyrslf.html

Helene G. Brenner, Ph.D. explains how to tune into your Inner Voice in *I Know I'm In There Somewhere: A Woman's Guide to Finding Her Inner Voice and Living a Life of Authenticity*, Gotham Books, 2003.

Christopher Germer advocates kindness and acceptance in *The Mindful Path to Self-Compassion: Freeing Yourself from Destructive Thoughts and Emotions*, Guilford Press, 2009.

2: Celebrate Your Survival Tools

Trauma is overwhelming by definition. To protect ourselves, we become numb to our sensations and emotions. Then when we notice ourselves at all, we criticize ourselves for the very behaviors that helped us survive through hard times. We want to leave behind these embarrassing souvenirs of struggle and become a perfect healing or healed person.

We can choose to honor ourselves for surviving and celebrate the tools that helped us make it through, including resistance, denial, dissociation, addiction, obsessive thoughts, and an Inner Critic. As we work to learn new tools, we naturally use the old ones less over time. Knowing that old tools remain available if we need them again, we feel safer to explore new ways one day at a time.

Do you have tools, patterns, or behaviors that helped you survive in the past, but are frustrating impediments now? What would help you respond to those behaviors with more compassion?

The Gift of Resistance

Resistance is usually labeled as a problem or even a character flaw. Instead, it can be treated as a gift of information from our deeper selves.

Change the focus. At the beginning of his bodywork session, a client courageously announced, "I didn't want to come today." When I invited him to explore his feeling further, he said, "I don't want to pay more attention to my pain. It claims too much of my life already."

Honoring this core truth, the focus of our session was on relaxation massage and noticing what is working in his life. He left the session feeling renewed and supported. His "resistance" carried an important message about what he needed in that moment.

Resistance comes in many forms:

- Procrastination on an "easy" task
- The urgent desire to be elsewhere
- Forgetting to do something
- Losing things, dropping things, generally being inefficient
- Sudden sleepiness
- Temper tantrums (for the younger set)
- Self-judgment — "I shouldn't feel this way."
- Self-sabotage — doing something even though "I know better."
- Your favorite resistance:_____

Notice judgment. In our earnest attempts to heal and become better people, many of us judge ourselves cruelly for our resistance in an increasing spiral of self-hatred and despair. "There's something wrong with me." "I must not want to heal." "I'm projecting my past onto this situation."

In my healing process, I find that when I feel the most stuck, my resistance contains the key to resolution and forward motion. When I finally stop trying to fix myself and surrender into the "unacceptable" feeling I have been fighting so hard, something shifts deep inside and I can move forward again.

Stuckness is acceptable. Even as I write this, wryly wondering why it takes so long to remember to surrender each time, I realize that the stuckness itself is part of the process, and not a reason for self-judgment. All my feelings are messages from my deeper self, even, or maybe especially, the ones I label "unreasonable".

Next time you notice that you are in resistance, try sitting with your feelings for a while, and attend to the messages they carry about your deep truth. Try giving yourself permission to feel exactly how you feel right now.

Tell a Story About Denial

Denial, the refusal to acknowledge a painful fact, thought, or feeling, is often judged negatively as a component of resistance. Being "in denial" is thought to be contrary, regressive, and the opposite of healing. We are urged to confront the truth, lose our illusions, and stop running away, all in the name of getting healthier.

Denial is protective. In fact, denial's primary role is protective, a circuit breaker for the psyche. When external events or internal responses overwhelm our resources, denial cuts off the overwhelming input to help us survive and keep us functioning.

Sometimes, one person's denial affects others around them, for example denial about addiction. The denial serves a protective role, and at the same time, others may need to express boundaries about the behaviors associated with denial. The possible external effects of denial are not addressed here.

Unawareness. There are different levels of denial. In the deepest level, there is no awareness that something is being denied. It takes tremendous energy to suppress all awareness of distress, and the information tends to leak out in unintended words, unexplained physical and emotional symptoms, and conflicted attraction around the denied information.

For example, an incest survivor may believe that she had an ideal childhood, but she sometimes surprises herself by saying negative things about her family, and she feels anxious and nauseated when she visits them. She may also be drawn to other survivors who are more conscious of their histories, without realizing the connection.

As we gather more resources over time, we are able to handle information that was previously overwhelming. We may also be drawn to investigate a denied area by the symptoms that arise.

Disbelief. This leads to the next level of denial, the cry of, "No! I don't believe that!" in response to new information. Now there is awareness of a battle with unpalatable information.

Disbelief slows the onrush of change to a bearable level, allowing us to move between the more familiar state of denial, and the newer informed state. We may move back and forth many times before we make all the adjustments necessary to stay with the new information.

Question hidden assumptions. The battle between awareness and denial can be frustrating and exhausting. It is possible that both sides are correct, if the denial is fighting against a hidden assumption that is unacceptable and untrue. For example, an incest survivor may fiercely deny that her family hurt her because the memories carry an associated toxic shame about being a bad person.

Tell a story. When you struggle with belief, it helps to explore the hidden assumptions around disputed or denied information. One way to do that is to write or tell a story about a fictional person who has the denied characteristics.

Set aside some time when you will not be disturbed. Set a minimum time to write, perhaps 5 minutes, or a length of time that feels right to you. Choose a comfortable location, and paper and writing instruments you like, or use your computer. You can also speak into a recorder. Bring some attention and energy to getting comfortable as you begin.

Name your fictional character and the information you are exploring. You can start with a mild version of the disputed information. For example, "Sometimes Tina's parents were mean to her."

Write whatever comes to mind and keep writing (or speaking) for at least the minimum time you set. Repeat, "I can't think of anything else to say," if you run out of ideas. If the words are flowing at the end of your allotted time, keep going until you reach a stopping point.

Set your story aside and take a break. Stretch, drink water, or do other activities that help you feel peaceful and centered.

When you are ready, go over your story slowly. Pause after each sentence and notice how your body feels. Are you tightening up, or relaxing? Are there any sentences that evoke a particularly strong reaction? Is there anything surprising to you? Do you get distracted or dissociate? The intention is to simply observe, rather than trying to change anything.

Remember to breathe and return to center as you complete the exercise.

In a few days, check in with yourself. How do you feel around the disputed information? You may want to do the story exercise again and notice if anything new arises.

Slow down change. Denial helps you heal by slowing down the changes required by new information and giving you time to adjust. Dr. Elisabeth Kubler-Ross named denial as the first of five natural stages of grief in response

to terminal illness or catastrophic loss.* Denial also protects you from hidden beliefs that are unacceptably damaging. When you embrace denial as a useful survival skill, it
smooths some of the struggle from your healing process.

---

* Dr. Elisabeth Kubler-Ross, *On Grief and Grieving: Finding the
Meaning of Grief Through the Five Stages of Loss,* Scribner, 2007.

Gain Awareness of Dissociation

Like denial, dissociation protects us from overwhelming input. Where denial distances us from a thought or feeling, dissociation distances us from our felt experience and body.

Dissociation can be short-term, such as listening to headphones and spacing out during a dental appointment, or long-term, such as feeling floaty and disjointed for months after a car crash. It can be local, withdrawing from a painful body part that has often received blows, or global, leaving the body entirely and remembering a difficult scene as if floating above it.

Growing up. Dissociation is one of the few tools available to young children to cope with trauma and abuse, especially if they lack a secure attachment to a parent or caretaker. Recurring trauma can eventually lead to compartmentalized awareness, a survival strategy generally known as multiple personalities. The formal label is Dissociative Identity Disorder (DID) or previously Multiple Personality Disorder (MPD).

Even without trauma, we are taught to dissociate from our bodies in many ways as we grow up. In search of approval, we learn to look to our parents, our teachers, our peers, and the media to find out how we feel and what we need instead of asking our own bodies.

Re-associating, becoming more present in our bodies, is a complex, worthwhile process. As we connect with what we feel in the moment, we can make choices that uniquely suit us.

Since disconnection happens for a reason, noticing it and thus beginning to reconnect may bring up strong emotions, thoughts, memories, or sensations. Proceed gently and slowly, and reach for support when you need it.

Noticing not-noticing. Noticing dissociation is difficult, since dissociation is all about not noticing what is happening. Indicators include feelings of vagueness, fogginess, distraction, or confusion. Other clues are walking into door frames, dropping things, forgetting appointments, or standing in a room wondering what your errand was.

How do you feel now? One way to track dissociation is to make a practice of asking yourself how you feel. Check in with yourself at least once a day, perhaps at breakfast, or after meditating. If you find it hard to answer, or find yourself thinking of something else instead, you may be disconnected from your body. Simply notice that for a few breaths.

Once you notice that you are dissociated, ask yourself if you want to reconnect further right now. If the answer is no, avoid doing anything that requires presence to be safe (using power tools, for example), and let the process drop this time. You have already taken a big step forward by noticing dissociation while it happens.

Reconnect. If you do want to reconnect, try one or more of these actions:

- Breathe deeply several times. Do your ribs move?
- Sense your feet. Push against the ground, stomp, or go for a walk.
- Put a hand over your heart, on your belly, or somewhere else that feels comforting.

- Drink water or tea.
- Sit in meditation for a few minutes.
- Anything that helps you connect with yourself.

Gently look back in time for events, sensations, emotions, or thoughts that might have triggered dissociation. Is there anything you can change about your situation to make it more hospitable for you?

As you begin to reconnect, you are likely to notice how disconnected you feel. This is an encouraging sign of progress rather than the defeat it appears to be.

Step by step. Even thinking about dissociation can be hard. Did you find yourself getting distracted while reading this? I had to re-focus several times while writing it. Dissociation is both an important survival skill and a frustrating roadblock when it does not happen by choice. Repeatedly, patiently noticing and reconnecting leads step by step to renewed aliveness, awareness, and enjoyment of life.

Addiction as Emotion Management

"[T]he realities of poverty, class, racism, social isolation, past trauma, sex-based discrimination and other social inequalities affect both people's vulnerability to and capacity for effectively dealing with drug-related harm." — Principles of Harm Reduction*

Addiction is a classic way to avoid or numb sensations and emotions.

Addiction is defined as physical and/or psychological dependence on a substance or behavior. Physical dependence leads to tolerance, where more of a substance is required to achieve the same effects, and to withdrawal symptoms when a substance is withheld. Addictions cause harm when they take priority over your well-being and the well-being of those around you.

Withdrawal effects. Sometimes withdrawal effects alone cause an apparent addiction. Many medications, including antidepressants and analgesics, have a rebound effect.** Stopping them abruptly causes a spike of symptoms, driving continued use of the medication. Tapering off can help prevent rebound effects.

Food intolerances can also cause a spike of detoxification

---

* Harm Reduction Coalition, "Principles of Harm Reduction." www.harmreduction.org/section.php?id=62

** The Icarus Project, "Harm Reduction Guide To Coming Off Psychiatric Drugs & Withdrawal." theicarusproject.net/HarmReductionGuideComingOffPsychDrugs symptoms when the food is stopped, driving continual consumption. If you have symptoms of an intolerance or sensitivity, look carefully at the foods you eat all the time.

Trauma bonds. Survivors of childhood abuse and domestic violence often struggle with obsessive relationships. When love and abuse are twisted together, they create powerful trauma bonds which look like an addiction to abusive relationships. The bond makes it as painful to leave the relationship as it is to stay. As you build a strong connection with your self, you will redefine love to exclude abuse and gradually leave trauma bonds behind. Give yourself kindness when healing takes longer and hurts more than you expect.

Harm to your self-trust. Both physical and psychological dependence lead to cravings. It is difficult to trust your internal signals when you crave something that causes harm. Rebuild self-trust by continuing to look within for guidance and including past consequences of your choices in your decisions. Cravings may have a sense of slipperiness or imbalance that helps you recognize them.

Reduce the harm. We receive a lot of messages that label addicts as bad people and addiction as a moral failure. Rather than label behaviors or people as unacceptable, the Harm Reduction Coalition advocates a more compassionate approach:

- Meet people where they are now.
- Reduce the harm of drug use.
- Help people meet their needs.

It is natural to want to numb, soothe, and avoid emotional and physical pain. At times, using a drug or other addictive behavior may be your best available choice to meet those needs. You can reduce the harm by having compassion for your choice. As you seek out more resources, your choices will change.

When your addiction feels compulsive or out of control, you can change your routine in some small way or add a small delay. Observe the compulsion as it moves through you. Sense how your body responds. What needs are met? What needs are still there?

Meeting ourselves now, in the present, with our present behaviors, is the only leverage point for change and the only entry point for compassion.

Remembered as overwhelming. An event is traumatic when it overwhelms our available resources. It can leave behind not only intense terror, rage, or pain, but also the imprint of feeling overwhelmed. Even after the traumatic event has ended and more resources are available, we continue to avoid emotions that are remembered as overwhelming.

Emotions are made up of physical sensations and energy inside you. What sensations are connected with specific emotions for you? For fear, you might notice shallow breathing and tightness in your belly. The following techniques can help you manage your emotions.

1. Dial down the intensity. Imagine a dial marked from 0-100 which controls the intensity of your emotions. Start at 0, with emotions completely suppressed. Turn the dial up slightly, to perhaps 3 or 5, and notice how that feels. Any time you feel overwhelmed, you can turn the dial to control the intensity of your emotions.

The dial helps you explore the edges of an emotion rather than jumping into the middle and getting flooded. A small amount of emotion can be surprisingly tolerable.

If the dial and the following techniques do not have any effect, you might be resonating with someone else's emotions, since your tools will not work on their emotions. Just considering the possibility can bring relief.

2. Give emotions more room. Many people learn to keep emotions tightly compressed in their bodies as tiny children. Back when our nervous systems were still forming and we had few coping skills, almost any emotion was overwhelming, especially if our parents did not model effective emotion management.

To feel the extent of your adult body, wiggle your fingers and toes. Stretch through your heels and feel the length of your legs. Take a deep breath and feel the width of your torso. With the intensity dial at a comfortable level, allow emotion to expand through your whole body. Some blocks take time to dissolve. You may feel places where emotion can expand and others which are still blocked.

It takes a lot of work to keep emotions compressed. It is less work and lowers the intensity of emotions when you give them more room.

3. Let the wave flow through you. Emotions are meant to move through us, flowing and ebbing like ocean waves. With the intensity at a comfortable level and as much space available in your body as possible, allow your emotion to flow. Notice how your sensations change as it swells and recedes. Does a different emotion arise? Watch it move as well.

Honor your choices. As you learn new techniques to manage your emotions, some addictions will fall away. Others may need professional intervention or attendance at a twelve-step group to resolve over time. Wherever you are in that process, reduce the harm as much as you can and honor your choices in the moment. You are doing the best you can with the resources you have available.

Behind the Curtain of Obsessive Thoughts

Whether we struggle with our bodies, our relationships, our addictions, or some other intractable problem, many of us find our thoughts cover the same painful ground again and again. We are not gaining new insights, and we cannot seem to stop the cycle. The thoughts themselves become a topic of worry and self-judgment.

Peek behind the curtain. In their book *When Women Stop Hating Their Bodies*,* Jane Hirschmann and Carol Munter explain that "bad body" thoughts are never about the body. Instead, they serve as a curtain to hide underlying issues that have been labeled "unthinkable." Not only are "bad body" thoughts (or any other obsessive thoughts) painful in themselves, but they leave the "unthinkable" issues unaddressed and unchanged.

Their process of noticing, questioning, and putting aside "bad body" thoughts can be adapted to any recurring painful theme. Over time, the theme occurs less often, and the underlying issues are gradually addressed.

1. Name a theme. Perhaps a recurring theme comes to mind immediately. If you cannot think of one, it is possible that a theme runs below your conscious awareness. For example, body hatred is so common that it becomes unnoticed background noise. Choose some reminder to check in with

---

* Jane R. Hirschmann and Carol H. Munter, *When Women Stop Hating Their Bodies*, Ballantine Books, 1995.

yourself — every time you enter your home, for example — and notice what you are thinking about over the next few days.

If you have several themes taking turns in your thoughts, choose one, perhaps the one that seems easiest to address.

2. Kind observation. Once you select a theme, simply observe when it comes up in your thoughts. "Ah, there it is." The more often it comes up, the more chances you have to watch it, so there is no need to judge the frequency of the topic in your thoughts. If judgment does arise, neutrally observe that as well.

At first, you may find yourself deep in the familiar obsessive pattern before you remember to step back and name it. After some practice, the first few words or images will be enough. "Ah, there it is."

3. Explore context. The next step is to explore the context that triggers the recurring theme. With kind curiosity, look back at what you were doing, thinking, feeling, and noticing just before the recurring theme started. At first, you may get repeatedly distracted, but eventually a pattern will emerge. Often a sense of relief and rightness accompanies the discovery. Sit with it and breathe.

You may need to notice and explore the context around your theme many times before a clear resolution appears. If frustration or other feelings arise around the process itself, bring your attention to them. Perhaps these emotions carry the message you seek.

4. Think the unthinkable. The previously unthinkable issue may be much bigger or much smaller than you feared. Sometimes, simply noticing and allowing a previously disallowed feeling — shame, or anger, or joy — resolves the problem. Sometimes, embracing a previously disallowed thought entails years of gradual action. "I never wanted to be in this career. I want to find out how I can contribute to the world." Sometimes, the uncovered thought heralds a big change. "I need a divorce!"

5. Reclaim your energy. Naming the underlying issue does not oblige you to make any immediate changes. The issue has been there all along, and simply acknowledging it is already a big step. As you reclaim the energy that was previously diverted into the obsessive thoughts, you may notice new ideas and plans bubbling up. Welcome them, and take action when the time is right for you.

Peace and power. The process of questioning and setting aside obsessive thoughts brings peace and power. Unchanging, painful thoughts are gradually replaced with awareness of underlying issues that have real solutions.

Calm Your Inner Critic

Have you noticed an ongoing commentary in the back of your mind that points out every mistake, omission, and fault you made or might make, including using your other survival tools? Most of us have it, commonly labeled the Inner Critic. You may have already noticed that arguing with your Inner Critic only leads to louder criticism, possibly about how self-critical you are.

Here are some reasons that voice exists, and some ways of moderating its harshness so that its positive effects can come through.*

Rules to stay safe. As we grow up, we internalize behavioral rules to keep us safe and save us from embarrassment. From "wear matching socks" to "stop at red lights" to "avoid him when he's drunk," our rules help us navigate a complex interpersonal world. The Inner Critic initially plays a helpful role by reminding us of the rules and making sure we follow them.

Frozen in time. Problems arise when our rules become frozen in time, as can happen with unresolved trauma. If "avoid him when he's drunk" comes from growing up with an abusive alcoholic, it may not apply to the company holiday party. The party stops being fun if the Inner Critic starts

---

* Robyn Posin's article "Criticizing Yourself," about making peace with her inner Hatchet Lady, is the source for some of the ideas in this article.
www.forthelittleonesinside.com/mpage/critself.html

2: Celebrate Your Survival Tools

wildly criticizing clothing, behavior, and everything else in an attempt to get out of there.

Agitated nervous system. Unresolved trauma also raises the activity level of the nervous system, so that the body is continually prepared to take emergency action. This leads to a feeling of, "Something is wrong!" and the Inner Critic steps in with an urgent rundown of mistakes and failings in an attempt to explain the feeling and fix the problem.

Much of the Inner Critic's severity comes from concerns about safety, as well as the urgent need to be heard. When you notice the Inner Critic's voice, you can kindly inquire into the underlying reason for panic. Awareness grows gradually as you work backward from the effect to the trigger.

1. Notice your body sensations when the Inner Critic is active. Does your stomach hurt? Are your shoulders hunched? Do you feel ashamed or defensive?

2. Listen for messages. As these sensations become familiar, listen for messages behind the sensations. Sometimes these messages are shockingly abusive, using insults we would never allow from others. Rephrasing the messages in respectful language offers the Inner Critic a broader range of tools for communication, as well as affirming your right to respectful treatment.

3. Attend to the situation. Once you hear the Inner Critic's messages clearly, pay attention to the situation that triggers them. Ask inside about what is frightening and what needs to happen to make the situation less frightening. Make it a priority to take thoughtful action on the information you receive even if it appears to be all about the past, since it is impossible to tell in the moment. Maybe that co-worker does behave badly when he is drunk, and it really is time to leave the party.

As your Inner Critic gains confidence that you are paying attention and keeping yourself safe, there is less need to yell so loudly or abusively. As communication improves, the Inner Critic will also thaw out some of those frozen rules and respond more to the present than to the past.

Quiet the nervous system. While you establish communication with your Inner Critic, consider adopting a physically calming activity as well. As your nervous system quiets down with yoga, meditation, bodywork, or some other activity you enjoy, the feeling of impending doom is reduced, and the Inner Critic, with less to explain, also quiets down.

What to do Right Now. Both of the previous suggestions can take months to bear fruit. When interactions with the Inner Critic spiral into paralyzing anxiety, an immediate intervention is needed.

For me, the magic words are "I am already doing the right thing." This simple sentence creates quiet out of chaos and gives me room to notice what I want to do next.

It also opens the door to viewing situations in new ways. As I explore the possibility that I really am already doing the right thing, I notice ways in which that is true, and my Inner Critic calms down. After all, her goal is to make me do the right thing. If I am already doing that, she can relax and does not need to yell at me. It is a relief all around.

Try it for yourself. "I am already doing the right thing." Breathe it in. Believe it for a moment, and allow yourself to explore the ways in which it might be true. How does your body respond?

Gain an ally. Converting the Inner Critic from enemy to ally leads to huge improvements in quality of life. As you tune in to internal signals, you will turn old rules into a flexible set of guidelines for making choices that work best for you. You will be well rewarded for the patience and work required to make the shift, as brief moments of calm turn into long stretches of peace.

Resources

Byron Katie has created a simple, powerful system for identifying and questioning assumptions called The Work. www.thework.com/thework.asp

In *The Obsidian Mirror: Healing from Childhood Sexual Abuse*, Seal Press, 2003, Louise Wisechild documents her process of remembering abuse and re-association in vivid, engaging, sometimes disturbing detail.

Twelve-step groups offer fellowship and assistance for people recovering from various addictions. Some of the choices are Alcoholics Anonymous (aa.org), Narcotics Anonymous (na.org), and Codependents Anonymous (coda.org). Using a similar model, Survivors of Incest Anonymous (siawso.org) offers fellowship and assistance for survivors of childhood sexual abuse.

The Icarus Project publishes a free 40-page guide online: "Harm Reduction Guide To Coming Off Psychiatric Drugs & Withdrawal."

theicarusproject.net/
HarmReductionGuideComingOffPsychDrugs

In *Riding Between the Worlds*, New World Library, 2007, Linda Kohanov discusses emotional congruence, emotional resonance, and emotional skills. Horses and sensitive humans are more comfortable around emotional congruence.

In their article "Hold That Fat Thought," Jane R. Hirschmann and Carol H. Munter explain their process for examining body hating thoughts and discovering their underlying message.

www.overcomingovereating.com/Feb94.html#hold

When Women Stop Hating Their Bodies: Freeing Yourself from Food and Weight Obsession, Ballantine Books, 1995, Jane R. Hirschmann and Carol H. Munter cover their compassionate approach to overcoming overeating in detail.

Robyn Posin passionately advocates for caring for our inner children with kindness. Her website has been an inspiration and a resource for many years.

www.forthelittleonesinside.com

I enthusiastically await Robyn Posin's forthcoming book *Go Only as Fast as the Slowest Part of You Feels Safe to Go: Tales to Kindle Gentleness and Compassion for Our Exhausted Selves.* See her website (above) for publication information.

3: Connect with Your Self

When we have enough safety, time, and energy, we can re-place our survival tools with new tools to compassionately observe and reconnect with our selves.

Meditation is time set aside to practice noticing thoughts, emotions, and experiences with neutral kindness. We can bring that kind attention to all our inner voices, as well as our "negative" experiences, including pain, longing, needs, and sensitivities. As we look inward with curiosity rather than fear, we suffer less. Paradoxically, observing our present selves with acceptance brings us the energy and clarity to meet our needs and make changes to care for our sensitivities.

Check in with your willingness to connect with your self. You may notice a mixture of calm readiness, strong emotions, vivid sensations, and sudden distractions.

Meditation: Safe Space for Noticing

Meditation creates a safe space to re-establish contact with our bodies and notice what is happening in the moment, including distraction, dissociation, and unwillingness to notice. Everything is accepted without judgment, including judgment.

I had thought that meditation required physical stillness and a quiet mind. It was a revelation to encounter Zen Buddhist Cheri Huber's non-threatening introduction to meditation in *How To Get From Where You Are To Where You Want To Be*.*

There, you're meditating! She writes (paraphrased): Sit comfortably, take three slow breaths, and notice what happens. Okay, now do it again. And again. There, you're meditating!

Five minute experiment. When I first read her book, my life was full of crisis and change. As an experiment, I committed to five minutes of meditation every morning for a month. It gave me a small island of steadiness in a sea of change. At the end of the month, I knew I wanted to continue.

Do you feel drawn toward exploring safe space for noticing? Check in with yourself about committing to daily five minute meditations for a specified length of time: a week, a month, or even just a couple of days. Try it and notice how

---

* Cheri Huber, *How To Get From Where You Are To Where You Want To Be*, Hay House, 2000.

you feel about continuing once the experiment is done. If you are already an experienced meditator, consider giving yourself even more permission to notice and embrace your actual experience in your practice.

Keep time. In a formal group setting, someone keeps time and rings a beautiful bell or chime to alert you to the end of the meditation period. When practicing on your own, you can use a timer or alarm, or take occasional peeks at the clock. It is surprising how five minutes can stretch out or pass in a flash on different days.

Two intentions. There are only two instructions for this type of meditation. Both are intentions to carry with you as you meditate, rather than requirements for being successful:

- Sit (or lie or stand) with your spine aligned.
- Count breaths from one to ten, and then start over at one.

Choose a position. Look around for a location that feels sheltered and comfortable for your meditation experiment.

You may want to sit upright on a chair, sit cross-legged on the edge of a pillow, or kneel with a larger pillow supporting you. Perhaps full lotus position, cross-legged with each foot resting on the opposite thigh, works for you. Standing, lying down, and sitting on the bed under the warm covers (my favorite for winter mornings) are also options.

You can allow your eyes to close, or keep them open with soft focus. If you are not sure which you prefer, try it both ways. Which is more comfortable for you?

As you practice, notice what sitting (or lying or standing) with your spine aligned means to you. Is it easy to let the top of your head float upward with solid support from your lower body? Do you notice any uncertainty about how to find alignment for your body? Notice what arises for you.

Count breaths. After settling into position, bring your awareness to your breathing. How do you know that you are breathing in or out? Do you hear the breath, feel the air move in your nose, or feel your chest or belly move?

The goal is to notice your breathing rather than trying to breathe in any particular way. As you breathe in, count "one" in your mind. Follow the breath in, and out. As you breathe in again, count "two". Continue to "ten" and start over at "one".

At some point you will probably realize that your attention has drifted to your thoughts, and you are no longer counting breaths. Neutrally note "thinking," and begin again at "one". Whether you count breaths in smooth cycles of ten, or never make it to "two," you are still meditating.

Notice your body. As you count breaths, you may notice sensations from your body: warmth, cold, tightness, ease, numbness, prickling, aches, releasing, shifting.

You may feel impulses to move or change position. Notice what those impulses feel like for you. Notice what happens if you choose to follow them, and if you do not. Remember, this is safe space for noticing. You are still meditating, no matter what choices you make.

Intense restlessness can arise even in a five minute meditation period. Notice what happens as you sit with the restlessness and wait for the meditation time to be over. Since this is all an experiment, you also have the option of ending early. Notice how it feels to have that choice and how it feels if you exercise it.

Already doing it right. Over years of daily meditation sessions, my body has learned more about sitting in alignment, and I count breaths all the way to "ten" a little more often. I keep returning because day by day I learn how it feels to already be doing something right, and gradually I have brought that acceptance into the rest of my life.

I hope you enjoy your experiment with already doing something right.

Many Voices, All Valid

We all need validation. If everyone received the full acceptance and acknowledgment we require, I imagine the world would fill with an immense, sudden, satisfied stillness.

While growing up, too many of us were surrounded by invalidation instead. When conflicts arose, we learned to argue, defend, and prove our point, or perhaps to yield quickly to the person in power. When something went wrong, we pointed fingers of blame and fault. There was rarely room for exploring both points of view.

Internal voices. Most of us have internal voices which are not always in harmony. The conflict can be as subtle as a muscle holding tension while we tell it to relax, as common as having mixed feelings about a decision, and as clear as hearing entirely different messages from our Inner Critic and Inner Nurturer. Survivors of childhood trauma often hear from an inner child or children who respond as if the past is still happening.

Some survivors of complex trauma have internal voices with defined, separate personas (alters). Multiple personalities (DID/MPD) occurs on a spectrum. Alters can be fully co-conscious, in partial communication with each other, or entirely unaware of other alters.

Take a moment to notice your experience of internal voices. Is it quiet or noisy inside? Do you recognize discrete voices, or is there a fluid shifting of opinions? How do you, the one noticing, respond to internal conflict? How do other internal voices respond to you?

Familiar structures. We unconsciously reproduce familiar power structures when facing internal conflict. Many of us grew up in hierarchical families. Someone is right and gets to be in charge. Everyone else is wrong and must be corrected or silenced. External appearances are more important than internal integrity. Rules must be followed, not questioned.

Working partnership. It is easy to believe that an Inner Nurturer has your well-being in mind. Surprisingly, Inner Critics, terrified children, and tense, painful muscles are also doing their best to help you survive and thrive. Conflicts arise when voices have differing assumptions, memories, and skills, as well as limited views of the present.

Rather than create a hierarchy, you can treat all parts of yourself as allies. As you establish communication and look for common ground, all voices learn from each other. With multiple personalities, this can lead to integration with alters merged, or to a comfortable working partnership among alters.

Open negotiations. Inner Critics urgently need us to follow those unquestionable rules. When we open negotiations with them, we learn about what the rules are, whether they are outdated, and what the consequences might be of breaking them. While the Inner Critic's tactics can be unacceptably cruel, their concerns can highlight present-day threats. Close-up, some Inner Critics are unexpectedly young and scared.

Share skills. A terrified inner child may not understand that she is now safe from abuse. She might have been too busy surviving to learn how to soothe herself when upset. The adult self can help her perceive the present and share skills acquired in the intervening years. At the same time, the busy adult may have lost connections with sensations and emotions in the body that the child still holds.

Connect and ask. A tense muscle could be reacting to scar tissue, suppressed emotions, stored memories, a current injury, or a habitual posture. Rather than order the muscle to relax, try these options:

- Allow yourself to connect with the area directly and experience it from the inside.
- Acknowledge that tension exists for a good reason. It solves a problem or achieves a goal.
- Gently inquire if the muscle has a message or request for you. Wait with openness and notice any words, images, sensations, or emotions that arise.

You might receive emptiness or non-response. When you connect and ask, you change your relationship with your tense muscle even without a clear answer.

Validation. When we treat parts of ourselves as enemies, we feel surrounded by enemies. When we greet all parts of ourselves with kindness and compassion, we feel some of the validation, acceptance, and acknowledgment we seek. Over time, compassion spills over to reach the people around us. While we may need to express boundaries about their behavior, we understand that others are doing their best to survive and thrive just as we are.

Befriend Your Pain

Trauma often results in physical pain, both directly from the event itself and indirectly from ongoing tension. When we relate to pain as a friend bearing a message rather than an enemy to be feared, we reduce the suffering we experience.

Pain as an enemy. We often view pain as an enemy to be vanquished. We ignore it, medicate it, stretch against it, worry about it, hope it will go away, and try to figure out what we are doing wrong if it is still here. Most of all, we physically fight it by tightening our bodies in protest, which often extends and perpetuates the pain.

Sometimes we distance ourselves from pain and feel numb instead, losing contact with a specific part that hurts, or feeling distant from the whole body. The following process works for numbness as well as for pain.

Pain as a messenger. We often tell ourselves drastic stories about what pain represents: illness, injury, neglect, punishment. What if the pain is simply a messenger, asking for your attention? Set the stories aside and attend directly to the pain as a friend.

Choose to begin. You can befriend your pain as part of a meditation practice or as a separate process. The first time through, you will probably want some time and privacy. You can also check in with your pain briefly while standing in line, or on a walk, or any time you have a moment to breathe.

1. Acknowledge resistance. Take some time to notice your usual responses to pain. Gently notice thoughts, emotions, images, and stories. Receive them with compassion. Dealing with pain can be exhausting, frustrating, and frightening. Remember that you have been responding to your pain as best you can with the information and resources you have available.

As you consider bringing gentle attention to your pain, do you notice any avoidance or resistance coming up? Simply breathe with the avoidance and resistance, and include them in your circle of attention.

2. Notice the pain. When you are ready, bring your attention lightly to your pain. Notice your sensations. Is the pain monolithic, unchanging? Or does it intensify, fade, move, or pulse in response to your attention? If it flows from one place to another, linger with the relief in the first location before you follow the pain to a new place.

If you find yourself distracted or in need of a break, allow your attention to rest on the rise and fall of your breath.

3. Notice what does not hurt. Pain can hijack our attention, cutting us off from the rest of the body.

After you attend to a painful area for a while, bring your attention to an opposite non-painful area. If the left shoulder is hurting, attend to the right shoulder. If your neck is stiff, bring your attention to the base of your spine. If everything hurts, gently search your body for a place that hurts less right now.

What happens in your body as you rest your attention on this more comfortable place?

You might become aware of tension trying to hold the pain at bay. Sometimes tension releases when you connect with it, or sometimes it releases more slowly over time. Your awareness of tension is a step toward healing.

4. Listen for messages. When you are ready, let your attention flow back to the pain. Do you notice any changes in the pain, or in how you respond to it?

Are you feeling curious about what message the pain brings? You might be wondering if it is from the past or the present. Is it getting everything it needs to heal? What else would be helpful to it?

Sit quietly and notice any images, sensations, or impressions that come up. They may surprise you, or confirm what you already knew.

The messages may flash by in an instant, or repeat louder and louder until you acknowledge them. If you receive only silence, or confusion, or fear, notice that, too. The seeming lack of response may be the message itself. Like a small child, the pain may need to sulk about being ignored for so long before it is ready to reveal anything else.

As much as you can, set aside your hopes and fears, and simply listen. The pain may tell you about one or more of the following:

- Sensitivities to your physical or emotional environment.
- Your past, with a sense of hurting "forever" or "never" healing, which are flashback markers.
- Overall stress on your system (chronic pain).
- Hope and healing, as your body adjusts to moving in new ways.
- The need for care, signaling an injury (acute pain).

When the conversation feels complete, thank the pain for speaking with you, and honor your courage for reaching out to your pain in friendship.

Relief. Befriending your pain brings tremendous relief both physically and emotionally. Each time you shift from fear to curiosity in response to pain's messages, you calm your nervous system and build more trust and peace within your body.

Invite Your Longing to Tea

You can sit with and inquire into emotional pain the same way you can befriend physical pain.

When you feel longing for something, do you take immediate action? We often move reflexively either to fulfill a longing or to suppress it, rarely taking time to sit with the longing itself.

Are you willing to connect to your feeling of longing? Not the subject, not the thing longed for, but the feeling itself. If that feels too risky, you can connect to just a part of it, 70%, or 5% — whatever feels right to you. You can also set a time limit, or end the visit when it feels complete.

To prepare, brew your favorite flavor of tea with care. Consider setting a second place for your guest. Curl your fingers around your mug and breathe in the aromatic steam. Settle more deeply into your chair, allowing your body to receive support.

Invite your longing, or part of it, to join you. Breathe, sip your tea, and notice what you see, hear, and feel as your guest arrives.

Describe your guest. Does your longing have a shape, color, or texture? Is it a faraway whisper, only audible in rare stillness? Is it shouting constantly with obsessive thoughts? Does it buzz like a yellow-jacket and take bites out of what nourishes you? Perhaps it hums peacefully.

Where in your body does your longing live? Is it a physical pull, or ache, or warmth? Does it transfix you like a fish hook as you try to wriggle and squirm away from it? Does it drive you like a whip into fulfilling it? Does it rock you like a child?

Are you old friends, or strangers?

Refocus. Is your focus slipping away to the subject of the longing? Refocus onto the feeling itself. Breathe, sip your tea, and bring your spacious attention to your guest. Simply wait, and receive whatever comes.

Untangle the feelings. Longing can be braided with many other feelings:

- Shame/judgment – "shoulds" around longing and fulfillment
- Fear – of not having enough
- Anger – feeling thwarted or frustrated
- Regret – over paths not taken
- Grief – for what is lost
- Love – perhaps the source of longing
- Pleasure – in daydreams and memories

Perhaps there are whole stories entangled with this longing. What thoughts and feelings arise for you? Acknowledge each one, allow it to move through you, and then bring your attention back to your invited guest.

Conversation. Do you have anything to say to your longing? Does your longing have anything to say to you? Remember to breathe, and open yourself to the unexpected.

Say goodbye. As the visit comes to an end, are there any changes in you, your longing, or the relationship between you? What do you see, hear, and feel? Next time you meet, will you be able to perceive each other more clearly? Have you come to appreciate anything about your longing, and yourself?

Gifts of longing. Our longings reveal our desires, our vulnerabilities, and our priorities. Longing is a powerful, painful force, and, with quiet attention and acceptance, it forms a gateway to greater connection and freedom.

Needs Amnesty Day

Like longings, needs are often suppressed. Have you noticed the gauntlet a need has to pass through before it can be internally acknowledged, much less spoken aloud?

We have many requirements on our needs and how they are perceived:

- Reasonably sized
- Age-appropriate
- Achievable
- Approved by "Them", also known as your internal committee
- Bearable – some needs trigger old pain
- Consistent with other needs and beliefs
- Justified – maybe this is just a want, not a need
- Worth the possible drama when spoken

What restrictions and filters limit your needs?

Need for quiet. Once while receiving a massage, I found myself irritated by the music playing in the room. I needed quiet, but told myself I could tolerate the music. I tried to tune it out. Finally, I mentioned it to the massage therapist, and she immediately turned it off. Ah, I could relax.

It takes a lot of energy to subconsciously evaluate needs and keep the unacceptable ones hidden away.

Take the pressure off by declaring a Needs Amnesty Day. Turn off your filters and allow your needs to make themselves known without penalty. Invite them all, from the confident, sleek ones you fulfill every day, to the strung out, malnourished ones you would usually cross the street to avoid.

Set limits. You are offering space for them to breathe, time for them to speak, and the soft light of acknowledgment.

You do not have to figure out how to fulfill the needs, or even approve of them. Simply acknowledge that, in this moment, they exist. Are there any other limits you need to set to make it more comfortable to hold this event?

Discover your needs. You know best how to reach your needs and invite them to your Amnesty Day. You could set a timer for 10 minutes and write "I need..." over and over, completing the sentences without stopping. Perhaps you want to speak out loud, or in the privacy of your mind.

Perhaps you want to announce your event a week in advance to let the word get around, and watch your guests arrive quietly one or two at a time.

Look behind your judgments. Searching for more guests? Some of your needs may be hiding behind your irritations, considerations, and judgments about your current life and environment. Set the timer for 10 minutes and let your opinions flow onto the page without stopping your pen. You have permission to be negative! When you finish, read over your opinionated statements, and reverse them to check whether there are needs behind them, the way my need for quiet was hiding behind my irritation with the massage music.

Talk with your guests. On the day itself, take some time to greet each guest. Ask for their names, their ages, and anything else they want to share. What do you notice about them? Are there any you have not met before? Have some changed since the last time you saw them? They will not be offended if you take notes.

How do you react to each one? What happens in your body? Are any emotions stirred up, such as longing or anger? Which of your filters might have kept this need away, if it weren't Needs Amnesty Day?

As your Amnesty Day comes to an end, allow a few minutes of stillness to simply notice what arises for you. You may feel exhausted, energized, or somewhere in between.

Is there anything you want to do differently as you interact with your needs in the future? Would you hold another Needs Amnesty Day? What feels possible and exciting for you?

Separate from fulfillment. We often use filters to suppress our needs because we think of them as problems we have to solve. When we allow our needs to exist separate from our struggle to fulfill them, they bring us crucial information about ourselves and our environment.

Sensitivities: Your Self-Care Guide

My friend Dinh raises many varieties of small, colorful kil-lifish. He carefully adjusts the conditions in each aquarium to meet the needs of its inhabitants, and provides the food each fish likes best. After years of observing and learning about killifish, he can identify a fish's species, age, and general health at a glance.

At no point does he tell an ailing fish that it should be less sensitive to its environment, or that other fish like the conditions just fine, or that he finds it inconvenient to make adjustments. He simply works to provide the most comfortable environment for each fish. Unsurprisingly, his fish thrive.

Notice judgment. When we humans notice sensitivities to our emotional and physical environment, we often judge ourselves as being "too sensitive," or compare our tolerance to others around us. Sensitivities are often labeled as an illness or internal defect, for example celiac disease (sensitivity to wheat gluten) or environmental illness (sensitivity to scents and chemicals).

Move toward self-care. Sensitivities are a valuable guide to moving toward our ideal environment. While it seems easier to go along with what is convenient for everyone else, sensitivity symptoms provide the motivation to speak up and take action to meet our needs. Symptoms can include ongoing fatigue, chronic pain, digestive issues, respiratory issues, brain fog, irritability, anxiety, and depression.

Do you experience symptoms or emotions that indicate your environment is not ideal for you? Just as Dinh uses observation and small adjustments to care for his fish, you can observe your reactions and experiment with changes.

1. Deserving care. As you consider doing the steps below, notice your beliefs and emotions around treating yourself with tender care.

Many of us carry underlying beliefs about not deserving good treatment, especially if it involves extra effort from other people. The labels and associations around sensitivity can be frightening, and the thought of making changes can be overwhelming.

Gently notice whatever thoughts and feelings arise. Do any of the actions below feel possible? Is there a different action that is coming to your attention, now that you are thinking about the topic of sensitivity and care?

2. Find your Inner Nurturer, the internal voice who believes wholeheartedly that you always deserve the best of care, no matter what else happens. Your Inner Nurturer agrees firmly with the kindest person you have ever known, whether a beloved relative, friend, or story character.

3. Observe. The next step is neutral observation and record-keeping. There is no need for evaluation or judgment here, since you are simply gathering private data for your own benefit, recording possible triggers as well as your body's reactions for a week. Choose one of the following sets of triggers, or follow your intuition about what information would be useful for you:

- If you suspect that you have food intolerances or allergies, record everything you eat, including ingredients as far as you know them.
- If you noticed reactions to scents or chemicals in

the past, record exposures to those.

- If you think you might have pollen allergies, record when you spend time outside and note pollen levels in your area.
- If you tend to pick up emotions from other people, record who you spent time with and how that felt.

Also record your body's reactions, including emotions, troublesome symptoms and times when you feel healthy and energized.

4. Experiment. Now that you have observed and recorded for a week, do any patterns suggest an experiment? This can be any small change, avoiding one thing that might be a trigger, or doing more of one thing that is energizing.

This is a favor you are doing for yourself rather than an obligation. Take as much time as you need to prepare for the experiment and stop when you choose. Two weeks is a recommended length of time so that you can get past any withdrawal reactions in the first few days. Keep taking notes to help guide your decisions in the future.

At the end of your experiment, notice how you feel. You have the choice to continue with this change, or discontinue it. Keep track of how you feel after discontinuing it as well. Continue observing and experimenting until you find what works best for you. If strong symptoms continue, you may want to consult a doctor or naturopath for assistance.

Lifelong process. Finding your best environment is a lifelong process of observation and experiments. Even when you are not keeping written records, your sensitivities will remind you to stay aware of your environment and reactions, and your Inner Nurturer will help you move toward conditions where you thrive.

Resources

In *How To Get From Where You Are To Where You Want To Be*, Hay House, 2000, Cheri Huber demonstrates a more compassionate way of relating to ourselves, our problems, and our resistance with stories about her students and her own life.

The workbook *Finding Life Beyond Trauma*, New Harbinger Publications, 2007, by Victoria Follette and Jacqueline Pistorello, offers many metaphors and exercises for noticing pain avoidance and taking constructive steps toward change.

Explain Pain, Noigroup Publications, 2003, by David Butler and Dr. Lorimer Moseley, uses whimsical images and metaphors to explain the neuroscience behind chronic pain and show how to calm the nervous system to generate less pain.

The idea of sitting with longing itself comes from Tara Brach's book *Radical Acceptance: Embracing Your Life with the Heart of a Buddha*, Bantam Books, 2003. Highly recommended!

Non-Violent Communication (NVC), created by Marshall Rosenberg, is based on communicating feelings, needs, and requests. The Center for NVC website includes a list of needs which may help you connect with your needs. www.cnvc.org/Training/needs-inventory

Marshall Rosenberg's book *Nonviolent Communication: A Language of Life*, PuddleDancer Press, 1999, describes Non-Violent Communication in detail, with examples.

4: Recognize Abuse

As we connect with our emotions, needs and sensitivities, we become more likely to recognize abuse and put a stop to it rather than blaming ourselves and feeling trapped.

Abusive behavior is used to assert power and control over the victim. Some abuse is as blatant as physical or sexual assault. Most abuse is much more subtle, and even blatant abuse is often covered with victim-blaming. "If you hadn't done that, I wouldn't have to hurt you."

Naming abuse is a crucial part of healing. When we name victim-blaming, manipulation, double binds, emotional abuse, childhood neglect, and spiritual abuse, we carve out space to perceive ourselves as separate from the abuse and reclaim our autonomy and power.

Recognizing abuse is a gradual process. Remember to be gentle with yourself as you look at past and current situations with new understanding.

Demand Respect, Not Victim-Blaming

When I told people I had just broken up with my abusive girlfriend, several responded, "Have you looked at your part?" Since I had tormented myself for months doing nothing else, the question left me speechless.

More appropriate responses to the news would have been, "How are you feeling?" or "I'm so sorry you're going through that," or "That's awful! No one deserves abuse!"

We all want to believe that life is fair and we are in control. We work hard to behave in "good" ways to stay safe. Unfortunately, that leads directly to the belief that if victims had behaved differently, they would not be coping with bad news now, so it must be their fault. Our fear makes us fiercely judgmental of vulnerability and powerlessness in ourselves and others.

Victim-blaming reinforces abuse. Victim-blaming robs abuse survivors of crucial support after an assault. Even worse, it stops those who suffer in ongoing abusive situations from reaching out for help. Emotional abuse is reinforced by the idea that victims deserve it, focusing their energy on "improving" themselves rather than on ending the abuse.

The victim has priority. People abuse for many reasons, including the desire for control, feeling entitled, feeling provoked, and feeling trapped. None of those reasons make the victim responsible for the abuser's actions. A victim's first priorities are safety, support, and healing. Compassion for the abuser is secondary to compassion for the victim. Recommending forgiveness can contribute to victim-blaming and silencing those with less power. "If only you weren't so upset, there wouldn't be a problem." Forgiving is intensely private and happens in its own time. Yes, terror, shame, and rage can hurt the person feeling them, but more harm is done by suppressing emotions and pretending all is forgiven, especially with ongoing abuse.

Our culture is steeped in victim-blaming. From popular magazines and new age movies, from psychotherapists and religious leaders, we are surrounded by messages about how to gain control over our lives by losing weight, spending money, or thinking different thoughts. Our Inner Critic joins the chorus and tries to keep us safe by detailing all the ways we need to fix ourselves right now.

You are already enough. Amid all the bustle of "try harder," "try smarter," "try better," a radically different message occasionally appears. Instead of telling us what is missing, it tells us we are already enough. Instead of telling us which external authority to believe, it tells us to listen inside and trust what we already know.

What happens in your body, in your heart, in your thoughts, when you give yourself permission to imagine that you are already enough? What if you do not need fixing? What if you already have plenty of the next fix you are tempted to buy?

The respect you deserve. Think of a recent puzzling or disturbing incident. Perhaps a store clerk was unaccountably rude as you completed a purchase. Did you ask yourself what you did wrong and how to fix it? How does that feels in your body?

Now imagine telling a friend about it, and your friend

responds by supporting your right to feel the way you feel, telling you that your perceptions are accurate, and appreciating that you shared your experience. How does your body feel as you imagine it? This is the respect you deserve.

Consider demanding more respect in your life. Move away from messages that say you need fixing, and toward messages that say you are already enough. Remind yourself that you are responsible for only your actions, not someone else's. Ask your Inner Critic to notice which beliefs keep you safer in the long run.

Strength in owning vulnerability. It takes courage to push away the blaming messages and sit with ourselves just as we are. It can be frightening to acknowledge that there is no magical action to make someone else change, and many events are beyond our control.

At the same time, owning vulnerability gives us the strength to notice our responses in the present moment. Secure in the knowledge that no one deserves abuse for any reason, we take action sooner to withdraw from situations that cause us pain and find abuse-free ways to meet our needs.

"Trust Me!" and Other Red Flags

When you confidently expect respect from others, attempts at manipulation become more obvious and less effective. Ahmed hesitated. Since the car crash a year ago, he feels nervous as a passenger. "Last time I caught a ride with you, you didn't slow down when I asked." His friend Ethan responded, "Trust me! You worry too much. Let's go, we'll be late."

Ahmed recognized several red flags for manipulation in addition to his concern about safety, and declined the invitation. Red flags are small boundary violations which could be warning signs for larger violations in the future.

Red Flag #1: "Trust me!" Our emotions occur in the private territory of our bodies. Telling someone what to feel ("Trust me!" "Smile!" "Relax!" "Cheer up!") is a boundary violation.

Trust is earned, not commanded. It develops over time by taking small risks and noticing how they turn out. Ahmed had already tried riding with Ethan and noticed that he did not like the result.

Traumatic events shatter our trust in personal safety, in the environment, and in other people. Eager to heal and be "normal", we sometimes force ourselves to take bigger risks because we think we "should", or because we want to act as we would have before the trauma, or because someone else is pushing us to do it.

The most important component of trust is your trust in

yourself. Notice when risks feel small enough to take, and when they feel too big. Try allowing yourself to decline risks that do not feel right to you. Ask your friends to support you in healing your self-trust.

Red Flag #2: "You worry too much." Judgment and shame are handy tools for controlling people. We are trained from childhood to track what other people think and alter our behavior to elicit a positive response. Even subtle judgmental signals about our emotions can cause us to disregard them and do what the other person wants.

Worry, fear, anger, and other emotions are authentic responses to our environment. They almost certainly relate to the past as well as the present. They almost certainly differ from other people's responses in the same situation, because no one has the same body, neurochemistry, and history.

Make room for all your emotions. No matter how uncomfortable or inconvenient they are, emotions carry important signals about your truth. When people say your emotions are "too" anything, they are really talking about their own discomfort. As Robyn Posin clearly states, consider not being with them at such times.*

Red Flag #3: "Let's go, we'll be late." This statement combines two common manipulative techniques: time pressure to make a decision, and assuming the desired outcome.

When you feel rushed, overwhelmed, or confused, take a moment to breathe and check in with yourself. In a life-threatening emergency, a quick check-in will help you choose an appropriate action. In all other situations, you have plenty of time to reach a decision that works for you.

---

* Robyn Posin, "Too Much."
www.forthelittleonesinside.com/mpage/too.html

Connect with your body. To help you discover what you want, imagine first one decision, then another, and observe how they feel inside your body. The more you connect with your emotions and sensations, the more familiar you will become with your body's delighted "yes," appalled "no," and uncertain or mixed "don't know yet."

Red Flag #4: Lack of congruence. When someone's words, actions, body language, and emotions do not match each other, the lack of congruence is a sign of deception or unawareness. Ethan's commanding tone and dismissal of Ahmed's concern are not congruent with respect and caring.

The mismatch may be as obvious as saying, "I'm not angry!" through gritted teeth, or it may be a fleeting expression or emotional overtone that you notice only subconsciously. When your body says "no" even though everything looks fine on the surface, you may be responding to a subtle lack of congruence.

Skip the guessing game. Ethan may be treating his friend the way Ethan has always been treated, without intending any harm, or he may be aware that he is using manipulative techniques. Like Ahmed, you can take action to protect yourself as soon as you notice red flags, without waiting to assign blame or guess intentions.

Mistakes are allowed. Some people will look for your vulnerable areas in order to manipulate you, and they may succeed at times. This is not your fault. We all have buttons which can be pushed, no matter how hard we work to heal and be strong. You do not have to be perfect to deserve respectful treatment.

You may act on a lot of red flags and think you are "too sensitive" or alternatively you may look back after a painful event and realize there were red flags you missed. It is okay to make mistakes in both directions. When we expect ourselves and others to notice and take action on every red flag in order to avoid abuse, we are blaming the victim for the abuser's actions.

Permission to act. When you pay attention to red flags, you claim your power to choose, help your self-trust heal, and make room in your life for people who treat you with respect. Give yourself permission to look inside for your truth and take action when you are ready.

Step Away from Double Binds

Double binds are another tool used to display power and gain control over others. They occur in daily life and also in extreme abuse. Victims of double binds feel confusion, rage, and despair at their entrapment and apparent lack of options.

You can effectively counter double binds by taking a step back and releasing your feelings, fully describing the situation, and choosing among many courses of action.

A double bind is technically defined* as a situation where:

1. Explicitly, if you do some Action, you'll be punished
2. Implicitly, if you don't do that Action, you'll also be punished
3. If you bring up the contradiction, you'll be punished
4. You can't leave the situation.

For example, some doctors use their position of authority to put their patients in victim-blaming double binds.

1. If you go to the doctor with serious symptoms, you are told you should have come in sooner.
2. If you go to the doctor with mild or vague symptoms, you are labeled hypochondriac or drug-seeking.
3. If you point out the contradiction, you are labeled uncooperative.

---

* Paul Gibney, "The Double Bind Theory: Still Crazy-Making After All These Years," 2006. www.psychotherapy.com.au/pages/journal/TheDoubleBindTheory.pdf

4. You still need medical care.

Name and counter double binds. If you feel trapped, rageful, or despairing, you may be experiencing a double bind. Take a step back from the situation and find some time and privacy to release your feelings. After that, you will have more clarity to look at your options.

Describe. The first step in countering a double bind is to write down each part as specifically as you can, including conflicting commands, punishments, consequences of naming the contradiction, and inability to leave the situation.

If some part of the double bind is missing, you have already found a possible exit from the trap. Past experiences of double binds can trigger feelings of helplessness even if the current situation does not meet all the conditions.

Accommodation and escape. Once you describe a double bind, there are many options to address it, ranging from accommodation to escape. Each situation is different, and one or more options may apply at different times.

- **It's not you.** Remember, there is something wrong with the situation, not with you.
- **Question the statements.** Is it true that you'll be punished?
- **Redefine punishment.** To a child, withdrawal of approval feels intolerable. An adult can find other sources of approval.
- **Change the focus.** In some cases, you can productively direct attention outside the double bind. In the medical example, you could say, "Let's focus on present symptoms and ways to treat them."
- **Meet your own standards.** Since all choices

lead to punishment, make the choices that meet your own approval.

- **Look for allies** within the situation. In the medical example, are there supportive members of the doctor's practice?
- **Ask for help.** Name the problem to outside witnesses or authorities. Stay aware of your power as you ask for help, rather than sliding into a Victim/Rescuer Drama Triangle.
- **Get external support.** Seek out people and activities that help you feel strong and resilient.
- **Walk away.** It's a big world. Have faith that you can get your needs met in abuse-free ways. Keep looking for and creating those ways.

You might try one solution and then another, finding your own Middle Way between accommodation and escape. Perhaps you will tolerate a difficult doctor until you hear of a more sympathetic doctor across town.

When you could not break free. Double binds are used in ritual abuse and torture, where the victim does not have the power and resources to break free. Faced with contrived choices between harming others and being harmed themselves, victims do their best to survive the chaotic, arbitrary environment. Domestic violence can follow this pattern as well.

Once away from immediate danger, survivors struggle with feelings of guilt and helplessness. For relief, analyze the double bind and put responsibility for the outcome on the people who created the situation. Grieve for the helplessness of the past, and think of positive actions to take in the future. With time, self-forgiveness becomes possible.

Sometimes we carry internal double binds. For example, someone healing from domestic violence might say:

1. If I have many PTSD symptoms, then I'm broken and worthless.
2. If I have few symptoms, then the abuse wasn't that bad.
3. Naming the contradiction does bring relief.
4. It is hard to escape my own beliefs.

This case is only a full double bind while the contradictory beliefs remain unconscious. Once the double bind is articulated, it loses its force. Questioning beliefs and getting external support helps with internal double binds.

Tool for oppression. Double binds are familiar as a tool for oppression to anyone lacking power in our society:

- Children are threatened with punishment for telling about abuse or bullying. If they don't tell, the abuse continues.
- Women can be penalized in the workplace both for lack of assertiveness and lack of femininity, with no approved middle ground.
- African-Americans naming racist words and actions are told to "watch your tone" no matter how gently the racism is pointed out.

Tool for healing. Noticing and countering double binds helps you heal from past abuse, step away from abuse in the present, and handle petty power games in daily life. You can also bring awareness to any contradictory expectations you have of people with less power around you.

Emotional Abuse: You Deserve Better

Emotional abuse can be as obvious as name-calling and raging, or it can be so subtle you spend days wondering why you feel so bad. It can happen between intimate partners, parent and child, teacher and student, boss and employee, siblings, co-workers, friends, strangers, any time people are interacting. Usually, but not always, the person in a more powerful position is the aggressor.

Emotional abuse is a kind of bullying. Using words, body language, and other behaviors, the aggressor implies or says directly that the recipient is wrong, bad, defective, shameful, fault-ridden, blame-worthy.

If the recipient protests this treatment, the protests themselves are sometimes targeted for further abuse. The aggressor might say, "You're imagining things," or "No one else has had that problem with me," or "Sure, honey, I'll stop doing that," but nothing changes. Often, the abuse is intermittent, alternating with more respectful or even charming behavior.

Signs of emotional abuse include:
- You feel unexpectedly shocked or confused by someone's words or behavior.
- You spend a lot of time wondering what you did or said wrong.
- You spend a lot of time worrying about what to do or say next.
- You question your memory of recent events.

- You feel fear when someone approaches you, even though superficially you have a positive relationship.
- You feel shame after interacting with someone, even if you cannot name why.
- You increasingly think you are stupid or crazy.
- You are trying really hard, but the relationship is getting worse, not better.

Get support. If you notice even one of the above signs, then that environment is toxic for you. Here are some ways to get support and start the healing process.

Take a break. If at all possible, take a break from the environment that is hurting you so that you can get grounded, clear your head, and decide what to do next.

In some situations, you may decide you do not want to interact with that person any more. In other situations, the person might be providing something you need or want. You may decide you want to continue interacting, at least for now, or you may feel powerless to leave. Get as much support as you can to counteract the toxic environment.

Believe yourself. Emotional abuse is corrosive to self-esteem, making it hard to be on your own side. As much as you can, gently observe your feelings and thoughts, and tell yourself, "There is a good reason I feel this way." "I deserve good treatment." "Maybe I am not the problem here."

Break the silence. Talk about what is happening. If someone disbelieves, denies, or blames you for the problem, say, "We have had different experiences," and find someone else to talk to. Keep trying!

Find friends. Seek out people who enjoy your company and whom you enjoy. Notice when you feel good during and after spending time with someone, and visit with them more often.

Get healing. If the situation is ongoing and/or your despair and pain are continuing or getting worse, seek out supportive professional healing, such as bodywork or psychotherapy. It is an immense relief to be received with respect, supported to speak your truth, and encouraged to reconnect with your body.

Know what you deserve. This list does not include suggestions for ways to improve yourself, fix the aggressor, or smooth your relationship with the aggressor. Sure, learn more about communication if it interests you, and work on your childhood issues if they are in your way, but do not do it in hopes of deserving better treatment.

You already deserve to be treated with respect and consideration just as you are.

Grieve Neglectful Mothering

Neglect is a stealthy type of abuse, absence of care rather than presence of overtly abusive behavior. Parents of all genders nurture children, and neglect from any parent is painful. Our expectation that mothers are nurturing adds another layer of pain when a mother is neglectful.

Criticizing one's mother is usually labeled as both cliché and taboo. When someone does speak up, the responses often focus on analyzing or defending the mother, while neglecting the adult child's feelings once again. This article describes good-enough mothering, the effects of neglectful mothering, and the healing reached through acknowledgment and grief.

Neglectful mothering leaves a profound wound of absence. It is hard to name what is lacking, and even harder to question and heal the feeling of not deserving any better. If the mothering you received was not good-enough, you may notice a sense of recognition or longing as you read. You may also notice intense rage, grief, or despair. Take breaks if you need them, and receive your emotions and thoughts with as much gentleness as you can.

Attunement and mirroring. A good-enough mother is attuned to her child. She attends to the subtle and not-so-subtle signals the child gives her, and does her best to meet the child's needs. This includes noticing needs for closeness and space, an ongoing dance as the child grows and explores. Attunement feeds not only the child's daily needs, but also the deeper need to feel welcomed and important.

A good-enough mother notices and mirrors emotions like excitement or distress, giving the child a sense of being seen and acknowledged. She provides soothing and containment when emotions intensify. Over time, the child learns how to soothe and contain emotions, internalizing the mothering.

Note that good-enough does not have to be perfect. A good-enough mother may sometimes feel overwhelmed and yell at her child, but she soon comes back into attunement. She stays aware of her own needs, sets appropriate limits, and shares care of the child with other adults when she can.

Many ways to be good enough. Good-enough mothering is found in all cultures and environments, from rich to poor, from strict to lenient, from staying home to full-time employment. Children form nurturing bonds with fathers and other caretakers as well. With attunement and mirroring, children grow up feeling secure and loved in a wide variety of households.

Blocks to attunement. Unfortunately, not all women who give birth are capable of attunement and mirroring. Severe physical or mental illness or personality disorders such as narcissism can prevent attunement to their children. Some are sociopaths, truly not caring about their children (or anyone else). Some have not received enough nurturing in their own lives to learn how to nurture others.

Neglectful mothering can occur in any culture and environment. The problem may be invisible outside the home, adding to the child's distress and lack of validation. Some neglectful mothers allow or even perpetrate active emotional, physical, and/or sexual abuse. Whether or not there is additional abuse, neglect itself has many damaging effects.

Internalized neglect. In a neglectful home, children receive neither validation for internal needs and feelings, nor the tools to handle them. Nurturing is conditional on attending to their mother's needs, so children become externally focused on pleasing others. Lacking unshakable confidence in their own worth, they embark on an endless quest to deserve love. Not only are their needs and feelings neglected when they are young, but they internalize this neglectful style and continue to treat themselves the same way into adulthood.

"Needy" vs. "strong." Adult children of neglectful mothers carry a powerful longing for nurturing and acknowledgment, along with an explosive cache of unexpressed grief and pain. Deep conflict arises between the "needy" young voice looking for mothering, and the "strong" older voice of self-protection and survival. Neither voice seems to hold the answer, since both vulnerable neediness and inauthentic façades lead to painful, chaotic relationships.

Both voices hold parts of the answer. The needy voice is right about the need to learn the missing lessons of self-acceptance and emotional containment in order to safely release that cache of emotion. The strong voice is right that adults need to maintain clear boundaries rather than merge like infants.

Reparative experiences. Fortunately, self-acceptance and emotional containment can be learned a little at a time while maintaining clear boundaries. Every interaction which includes a little attunement or mirroring helps to heal the wounds left by neglectful mothering. Compassionate friends and helping professionals provide these reparative experiences.

You can create your own reparative experience right now.

Bring your attention to your next breath in, and out. Simply notice sensations and thoughts. Whatever you notice, say to yourself, "It's okay to feel/think that." Even if you do not notice anything (you might be dissociating), say to yourself, "It's okay not to notice anything." Everything you experience in this moment is okay, whether positive, negative, or neutral. This is attunement and mirroring, acceptance and support. This is your birthright.

As these reparative experiences accumulate, a more compassionate maternal voice grows inside. Gradually, it becomes possible to tolerate and even comfort the grief, rage, and pain at the loss of good-enough mothering. Through allowing and expressing those feelings, the old lessons of self-neglect are slowly replaced with abundant self-love.

Acceptance and support. Neglectful mothering leads to a terrible spiral of pain and self-judgment. The only way out of the spiral is acceptance and support. At first, these seem like empty ideas, but gradually external reparative experiences and support lead to internal acceptance, creating a new spiral of healing and joy.

Spiritual Abuse: Take Back Your Faith

Like neglectful mothering, most trauma has spiritual implications. "Why was I hurt?" "Why wasn't I protected?" "Do I deserve to have bad things happen?" It feels agonizing to believe that Spirit (God, Goddess, Allah, Elohim, the Grandmothers, the Universe, your Higher Power, your Deep Self, etc.) endorses the pain you endure. Survivors of spiritual abuse contend with a shattered connection to Spirit at the same time.

Harm from spiritual officials. Spiritual abuse occurs when spiritual officials (preachers, rabbis, shamans, etc.) use their power to harm their congregations. Blatant examples include ritual abuse*, where worship and horrific abuse are combined, and cults, which control their members' social, financial, and spiritual lives. Spiritual abuse can also be subtle, for example a minister who tells a woman to return to her abusive husband without concern for her safety, or who counsels gay and transgender youth to "pray to be cured."

Any religion or set of beliefs can be used for spiritual abuse. The abuse can be explicit in a congregation's ideology, such as believing that everyone must submit to the leader, or contrary to it, such as a priest sexually abusing children.

Damaged connection to Spirit. Spiritual abuse also

---

* For more information on ritual abuse, see the Survivorship Frequently Asked Questions page: www.survivorship.org/faqs.html

occurs when any abuser damages the recipient's sense of worth, purpose, or connection to Spirit. An abusive partner instills a sense of hopeless inevitability by repeating, "We were meant to be together." Parents continue a legacy of lives ruled by fear rather than joy when they control their children's behavior with threats of eternal damnation.

Spiritual abuse violates not only trust in the abuser, but also trust in Spirit. It breaks your connection with your right to exist and take up space. It is much harder to leave an abusive situation while convinced that you deserve abuse. It is much harder to heal afterward when the abuse feels like proof of your worthlessness.

Faith is what you know for sure. To heal, look inside for faith. Not for what you think you should believe, or for what someone says you should feel, but for what you know for sure without the need for external proof.

Reach inside for what you are certain of. What do you turn toward like a flower toward the sun? What do you long for deep inside, no matter how hard you try to ignore or erase the longing? Those longings tell you what you know you deserve.

Look inside for your urge to heal, the part of you that searches for solutions. Have you felt suicidal or hopeless and fought hard to survive? Somewhere inside there is a determination to live and thrive.

Faith is a private matter between you and Spirit, even when you worship with a congregation. When someone tells you what to believe without your consent, it is a boundary violation and a red flag.

Faith helps you choose beliefs. If a belief leads you into a spiral of doubt and pain, consider discarding it. Some people find it comforting to believe that they chose their parents before birth. I find it intolerable to believe that my deep self would intentionally cause me that much pain, so I dropped that belief.

Move toward beliefs that bring you relief, lightness, and a sense of renewed possibility. Faith tells me that I live in an abundant Universe and it is possible to get my needs met without abuse. This allows me to leave abusive situations and keep looking for new ways to meet my needs rather than believing it cannot get better.

Be wary if you find judgment and bargaining as you reach for your faith. For me, those come from inner voices mimicking what they think I should find. Faith tells me that judgment and bargaining have no place in my connection with Spirit. Underneath all the yelling and doubt, I find quiet, kind, steady compassion.

Your faith exists with or without your trust and belief. You might find an ever-burning flame inside and wonder if you dare to claim its power. You might find wordless support that scatters when you try to capture it, yet always returns. You might realize that you already have much of what you long for.

You deserve kindness. Each trauma survivor forges an individual peace with the coexistence of trauma and Spirit. Whether or not you have experienced spiritual abuse, I know without needing proof that you belong here and you deserve kindness, not pain.

Resources

Not Trauma Alone, Brunner/Routledge, 2000, by Steven N. Gold is an academic text with a profoundly respectful attitude toward survivors of prolonged childhood abuse. I wish every practitioner working with traumatized people would read and absorb this book.

Robyn Posin affirms that you are never too sensitive in her article, "Too Much."
www.forthelittleonesinside.com/mpage/too.html

Paul Gibney's article "The Double Bind Theory: Still Crazy-Making After All These Years," 2006, explores Gregory Bateson's original research on double binds in relation to schizophrenia and contains several extended double bind examples.
www.psychotherapy.com.au/pages/journal/TheDouble
  BindTheory.pdf

Patricia Evans's books are excellent sources of information about emotional abuse: *The Verbally Abusive Relationship*, 1996, and *Controlling People*, 2002, both published by Adams Media Corporation.

The Mother I Carry: A Memoir of Healing from Emotional Abuse, Seal Press, 1993, by Louise Wisechild explores the legacy of growing up with emotional abuse and shows how to come to peace with the present.

In *Will I Ever Be Good Enough? Healing the Daughters of Narcissistic Mothers*, Free Press, 2009, Karyl McBride describes the behaviors and effects of narcissistic mothers and provides a detailed roadmap for healing.

In *Leaving the Saints: How I Lost the Mormons and Found My Faith*, Three Rivers Press, 2006, Martha Beck shares her experience of spiritual abuse, longing, family, Spirit, and faith. Her memoir tackles these serious subjects with a light touch and humorous details.

Survivorship is an organization for and by survivors of extreme child abuse, including sadistic sexual abuse, ritualistic abuse, mind control, and torture. The website provides articles, frequently asked questions, difficult dates, and subscription information for their quarterly magazine of art and articles by survivors.

www.survivorship.org

5: Understand Post-Traumatic Stress Disorder (PTSD)

The process of healing from trauma varies from person to person depending on the length of exposure to traumatic events and the internal and external resources available to the survivor during and after the events.

Post-Traumatic Stress Disorder (PTSD) is defined as a set of symptoms which continue unabated after the trauma rather than resolving over time. PTSD is diagnosed when someone experiences:

- Intrusive memories (flashbacks)
- Avoidance and emotional numbing
- Anxiety and increased emotional arousal

All three symptoms result from the nervous system's natural response to overwhelming surprise and pain. Intrusive memories occur in an attempt to digest and process events that were too intense to process as they happened. Avoidance and emotional numbing effectively reduce pain to manageable levels. Anxiety and increased emotional arousal come from fear that the threat is not over, so the body remains prepared for action.

Healing from trauma remains possible even after years of symptoms. It helps to remember that progress is uneven. The hard times do not last forever, even though it feels that way while they are happening. You can connect with past trauma at a pace that works for you and learn new skills to handle flashbacks, anxiety, and the freeze response.

Suicidal thoughts and feelings are a common trauma response that can be hard to talk about. If you have a plan to harm yourself, please talk to someone even though it is hard. You deserve help, and you deserve to live. Listening to your thoughts and feelings without harming yourself can ease some of the emotional pain.

Understanding your body's survival mechanisms helps you cope with the problems they cause and move in the direction of healing.

Ups and Downs of Healing from Trauma

Many of us imagine that healing from the emotional effects of trauma is like healing from a physical wound. Each day, a healing wound gets a little smaller and less tender until it disappears. If a physical wound grows bigger or more tender at some point during the process, it is considered a setback and a sign for concern.

Stuck in a closet. By contrast, healing from trauma is more like slowly moving out of a cramped, crowded closet. During the traumatic event, the small enclosed breathless space feels life-saving. After the emergency is over, it can feel like a limiting, unending entrapment, where change is impossible and self-blame is very loud.

A physical state. There are physical changes in both brain function and hormonal activity that correspond to life in the trauma-reaction closet. The nervous system is highly agitated, leading to restlessness, powerful anxiety, and self-critical, racing thoughts.

Several key parts of the brain shut down, including the section responsible for perceiving the passage of time, and the part that allows for self-reflection.* Meanwhile, adrenaline causes shallow breathing, rapid heartbeat, and increased blood flow to major muscle groups. While the closet does not have physical walls, it is still a physical state.

---

* Dr. Bessel van der Kolk, "Clinical Implications of Neuroscience Research in PTSD."
www.traumacenter.org/products/pdf_files/NYASF.pdf

Healing comes from gradually processing overwhelming experiences so that the body realizes that the emergency is over.

Brief reprieves. As emotional healing begins, there are short visits outside the closet. The constant agitation of an over-stressed nervous system quiets down. Breathing expands all the way into the belly, and sighs out gently. The world sparkles with renewed color and detail. Hope arises for steady improvement.

Back in the closet after the short excursion is over, nothing has changed, including the feeling that nothing will ever change. The brief reprieve feels like an unrepeatable fluke, with the added despair of "backsliding."

Turning point. As emotional healing continues, the excursions lengthen and happen more frequently. A turning point comes when, back in the closet with feelings of timeless entrapment, the memory of being outside the closet is also present. Eventually, a brief stint in the closet becomes a reminder of how much healing has occurred, and how much better life usually is nowadays.

Practice the transition. When recovering from trauma, the goal is to remember how to make the transition from agitation to calm, rather than achieving a state of calm and never leaving it again. From that perspective, each sojourn in the closet, as uncomfortable as it is, gives an opportunity to practice the transition back into a more comfortable, calm state.

To make the closet more bearable:

- Remember that experiencing the closet does not represent a failure, nor a life sentence. It is a normal response to traumatic stress, and it will change with time.

- Give yourself permission to heal slowly, with a lot of back and forth between feeling better and feeling just as bad as you did before.
- Celebrate your strengths. List all the things you did to survive the original trauma and all the things you are doing now to survive the difficult time you are going through.
- Keep a mood log to help you track the changes you are going through. It can be on the computer or on paper, brief phrases or extended journaling. Read it over when it feels like nothing will ever change.
- Anxiety is often a big part of the closet experience. Make a list of all the ways you have learned to manage anxiety and bring peace into your life. Post your list in a prominent place, and refer to it often.
- Some people find help through medications. For people with sensitive systems, homeopathic remedies such as Bach's Rescue Remedy tincture or ointment can be helpful.
- Seek out support. Notice the people, events, and activities that help you feel calmer, and seek them out. Stay aware of the difference between calmness and numbness or dissociation. Numbness gives you a welcome break from feeling awful, but it will not help you re-learn how to become calm.

If you notice over time that you are still stuck in the closet as often as before, consider getting trained assistance in gently and gradually re-negotiating the trauma. EMDR (Eye Movement Desensitization and Reprocessing), Somatic

Experiencing, and neurofeedback have been shown to be effective techniques.

Give yourself time. As much as you can, observe the ups and downs of your healing process with kind curiosity. Luxuriate in the reprieves, endure the hard times, and above all honor yourself for surviving and healing from a traumatic experience.

Remember at Your Own Pace

Both childhood and adult trauma are sometimes suppressed completely until time and other resources are available to remember and heal.

When she was small, Yael's grandfather taught her to play the piano. After each lesson, he caressed her in uncomfortable ways and swore her to secrecy. When her family moved away, Yael left behind both her memory of being molested and her love of making music.

In her thirties, feeling aimless and depressed, she took up piano again and experienced an unexpected flood of emotion and memory.

Full range of memory. Trauma survivors experience a full range of conscious memory after the event, from complete details to complete amnesia. Memories return when it takes too much energy to keep them suppressed, or when an essential part of the self is buried along with the memories, and the remaining self gets lonely enough to start digging. Memories can come back suddenly and completely, or gradually over years, or anywhere in between.

Remembered helplessness. An event is traumatic when it overwhelms the coping skills available at the time it happens. When the healing process is also overwhelming, it adds to the trauma. While remembering trauma is not fun, it does not have to feel catastrophic.

Much of the distress of remembering is itself part of the past. The memory of being overwhelmed is stored along with the sights, sounds, and body sensations of the event. Returning memories can include a potent mix of disbelief, shame, fear, rage, grief, feeling conflicted, feeling inadequate, feeling like a failure, and feeling like nothing will ever be the same again.

Anything you remember is already part of you. You already survived it. It did end.

Manage a flood of memories. When memories return suddenly as flashbacks, the challenge is to contain the flood and remain aware of the resources you have in the present.

Put a frame around a memory, imagining that it is behind a window or on a small TV screen that can be muted or turned off. The frame puts a memory in context and makes the events less physically overwhelming. Your whole body can relax as it realizes that the threat really is over.

Time is an important resource. Unlike the original event, you can slow down the process of remembering to a manageable rate. You can choose when to invite a memory closer and when to put it aside for later. As your system learns to trust that you will give the memory your attention when you can, it will cooperate when you need to attend to the present instead.

When memories take a lot of your time, attend to present-day tasks in small increments. Think of it as a gift to your future self. If you wash one dish now, there will be fewer to wash tomorrow. At the same time, it is a gift to your past self, helping you connect with your present-day strengths and skills.

Many coping skills. In addition to time, you have many other resources that were not available to you during the traumatic event. Notice how your coping skills have grown since it happened. Not only are you confronting a memory rather than the event itself, but you have more resources available to handle it.

As Yael remembers being molested, she has a lot of resources she lacked as a child:

- An adult body that can defend her
- Friends who believe her
- Control over who she spends time with
- Communication skills to set boundaries and name what happened
- A home far from where the abuse happened
- Access to professional help
- Choice of when and how much to practice piano if it continues to trigger her

What resources do you have available to you now?

Manage a trickle of memories. Sometimes, memories hover below the surface for months or years, causing emotional and physical signs of trauma while remaining frustratingly elusive. The challenge is to connect with whatever information is available about the past.

Your psyche has good reasons for not remembering. Take some time to appreciate the self-protection and get curious about what those reasons might be. What would have to change to make it safe to remember?

Gather the fragments. When you gather the fragments you do have, they may add up to more information than you realized. You may be remembering sensory information from a time before you had words. You may be remembering confusion and disbelief. Your emotions about remembering, for example fear or frustration, may be pointers to the past.

You can say aloud, "I am willing to remember what

happened." Take note of any glimpses or impressions you get, no matter how unlikely. When you have more information, you may ruefully say, "Now I understand why I wasn't remembering that."

You can try the writing exercise suggested for exploring denial on page 35. You can also try writing or drawing with your non-dominant hand.

Allow yourself to doubt. Witness the images inside you without requiring that they match exactly with external reality. You are not looking for courtroom-level proof. You are exploring your personal language of images, sensations, and thoughts. They are there for a reason, even if they do not "make sense."

Doubt is part of the process. Your trust in your memories will probably veer from 100% to 0% and back again, sometimes rapidly. Allow doubt to come and go, and notice if anything specific triggers doubt for you.

Others may also doubt your memories. You can set boundaries around hearing other people's judgments or decline to discuss your memories with them further. You can also seek out people who support you in trusting your inner voice.

Take the reins. Trauma is overwhelming, but healing does not have to be. The sense of something wrong that must be fixed as fast as possible comes from the past, not the present. There is no time limit or race to be won in your healing. Take the reins and remember at a pace that works for you.

Flashbacks: Experience Distress in Safety

Flashbacks are one of the hallmark symptoms of Post-Traumatic Stress Disorder (PTSD). A flashback consists of intrusive sensations, emotions, and reactions from the past which impinge on a trauma survivor's present-day life.

Pedro spots his friend Hannah at a party. She has her back to him, so he touches her shoulder and greets her. Rather than turning and answering, she goes rigid for a few moments, then takes a deep breath and asks him not to touch her by surprise again.

For Hannah, the unexpected touch triggered the sensation of being violently grabbed on the shoulder during an assault. She felt a spike of panic, as if she were back in the dangerous situation. She was having a flashback, re-experiencing a traumatic memory.

Narrative and traumatic memory. Our nervous systems store ordinary, non-overwhelming experiences in the form of narrative memory, including a sense of time, place, and ourselves as narrators. When a narrative memory is remembered, it is clearly in past tense.

Memories are stored differently under extreme stress. Back when Hannah was being assaulted, her body was focused on survival, too overwhelmed to create narrative memories. Her nervous system stored traumatic memories instead: fragments of raw sensory data without the anchors of time, place, or narrator. Traumatic memories are remembered in present tense.

Traumatic memory: *Pressure on shoulder, sudden pull off balance, close-up of a milk carton, terror, draft of cold air, anger, beep of a cash register.*

Part of the healing process. In his self-trauma model,* Dr. John Briere proposes that flashbacks are part of the solution for PTSD, rather than a symptom. Each flashback helps defuse and integrate raw traumatic memory into less charged narrative memory.

The key is to experience the distress of the past within the safety of the present. If past distress entirely blocks out awareness of present safety, the effect is re-traumatizing rather than therapeutic.

Recognize flashbacks. When a traumatic memory fragment is recalled, the lack of context makes it hard to distinguish from current sensory experience. Some flashbacks contain emotion (terror) or internal sensation (shoulder pain) without accompanying images or sounds.

Flashback signs:

- Strong reaction — a response that is unexplained by current events.
- Timelessness — a sense of "always", "never", or "forever."
- Disorientation — confusion about current dates, times, places, or people.
- Helplessness — feeling overwhelmed, powerless, panicky, or trapped.
- Changed self-perception — feeling smaller or younger.

---

* John Briere, "Treating Adult Survivors of Severe Childhood Abuse and Neglect: Further development of an integrative model." www.johnbriere.com/stm.htm

With practice, you will become familiar with your internal signs of a flashback and recognize them more quickly.

Respond to flashbacks. When you notice signs of a flashback, the following tools can help:

- Notice your experience in the moment. Your attention begins the healing process.
- Validate your response. Whether you are responding to the past or the present, your emotions and reactions are real.
- Ask yourself if your experience is old or familiar. Sometimes simply naming a flashback reduces its intensity.
- Orient to the present. Look around, say the date, say your age.
- Ground yourself. Take a deep breath, stamp your feet, drink some water.
- Remind yourself that it ended. Whatever you are remembering, you survived it, and you are safer now.
- Take gentle care of yourself. After the flashback ebbs, you may feel raw and fragile for a while. I call this a flashback hangover.

Manage triggers. Pedro's touch on Hannah's shoulder was a trigger: a current sensation, emotion, or thought which leads to a flashback. Triggers are usually similar to the traumatic memory in some way, but the connection is not always obvious. The time of year, a faint scent, or a fleeting thought could be triggers.

When you experience a lot of flashbacks, avoiding triggers helps establish safety and gives you a chance to rest. When you feel calmer and stronger, you can gradually expand your horizons and re-introduce some triggers. Establishing a foundation of safety is crucial for healing.

Healing in action. Since she has had a lot of practice, Hannah could observe her intense reactions, name them as a flashback, and remind herself that she was safe at a party. As the reaction ebbed, she could tell her friend how to avoid that trigger in the future.

By experiencing the distress of a flashback within the safety of a party, she has taken another step toward processing traumatic memories and integrating them into narrative memory: *Two months ago, I went to the store to buy milk, and someone grabbed my shoulder.*

Take pride in your process. Flashbacks often contain wrenchingly painful material and interfere embarrassingly with daily life. At the same time, they are a sign of your body's wisdom reaching for healing. Remember to take pride in your survival, your current safety, and your strength as you confront and heal from past trauma.

Anxiety, Your Relaxation Coach

Anxiety is a natural response to traumatic events and a primary symptom of PTSD. Physically and psychologically, we worry that a threatening event will happen again, and no longer feel as safe.

Braced shoulders, worried thoughts, shallow breathing. Leila notices her signs of anxiety and pauses to acknowledge them. Her quiet attention interrupts the rising anxiety and allows her body to relax instead.

Chronic anxiety arises from a variety of causes, not all related to trauma:

- Physical sensitivities
- Neurochemical imbalances
- Current stressors or danger
- Resonance with other people's anxiety
- An over-active Inner Critic
- Physical pain
- Flashbacks to long-past anxiety
- Ups and downs of healing from recent trauma.

Anxiety comes from an imbalance between two parts of the nervous system. The **sympathetic nervous system** is responsible for fight, flight, and freeze reactions. It increases stress hormone production, increases sweating, accelerates the heart rate, dilates the bronchi in the lungs, and inhibits salivation and digestion. When the sympathetic nervous system is dominant, we experience **activation**: tension and

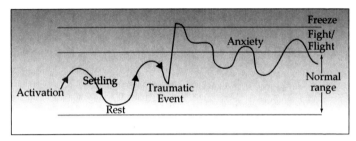

Figure 1: Nervous System Activation Over Time

increased stress.

The **parasympathetic nervous system** is responsible for rest and digestion. It does the opposite of the sympathetic nervous system: increases salivation and digestion, decreases stress hormone production, decreases sweating, slows the heart rate, and narrows the bronchi in the lungs. When the parasympathetic nervous system is dominant, we experience **settling**: relaxation and decreased stress.

Everyday activation. We all experience alternating activation and settling as we go about our days. For example, Leila's heart rate increases before an important meeting, keeping her alert and focused. Afterward, she relaxes as she eats lunch. Later, she experiences the activation of exercise as she rides her bike home.

Emergency activation. A threatening event triggers immediate activation into a full fight or flight response. If the nervous system perceives an overwhelming threat and no possibility of overcoming it, even more activation results in a freeze response. Incomplete settling after activation results in anxiety. See Figure 1, above.

When a car pulls out in front of Leila as she rides, she swerves and brakes thanks to her sympathetic nervous system. After successfully avoiding a crash, she needs time to tremble and discharge the stress. If she does not have a chance to settle completely, or if she has had past close calls or crashes, she may experience a spike of anxiety the next time she plans to ride her bike.

Accumulated responses to past trauma can result in chronic anxiety. Physical signs include shallow breathing, braced muscles, being easily startled, stomach in knots, chronic pain, and insomnia. Psychological signs include spiraling worry and negative thoughts, sometimes culminating in panic attacks which can feel like heart attacks.

Unless interrupted, anxiety reinforces itself. Physically, the sympathetic nervous system stays more active and suppresses the parasympathetic system. Psychologically, we become anxious about the physical signs and about the anxiety itself. The following tools can address anxiety.

Interrupt anxiety with acceptance. When you notice signs of anxiety, pause to acknowledge them. Name them in a neutral way. "Braced shoulders. Worried thoughts. Shallow breathing." Remind yourself that anxiety is simply activation, your body's way of preparing for a possible threat. Thank your body for protecting you.

Meet physical tension with acceptance. You do not have to like it or enjoy it, but in this moment, these particular muscles are tense. You may find that they relax when you acknowledge them, or they may stay tense. Either way, at least you do not have the additional discomfort of fighting your body.

Change your story. Leila is meeting friends for dinner, and they have not shown up. Anxiety says, "They forgot! Or I'm in the wrong place!" She notices her worried thoughts, and creates a more peaceful story. "They're running late. They'll be here soon. If not, I'll call in a few minutes and enjoy dinner on my own." Whether they arrive or not, she experiences a more pleasant wait.

If you notice thoughts focused on what you are doing wrong, try a new question: "What am I doing right?" You are probably doing several things right, and suddenly the world will seem less threatening.

Celebrate settling. Signs of settling include a spontaneous deep breath, stomach gurgling, muscles relaxing, shifting to a more open posture, and feelings of ease and well-being. Notice how settling feels in your body, and enjoy it when it happens.

Remember your exits. Take note of activities and thoughts which help you exit from an anxious state. Do more of what you find calming. You may also want to investigate non-trauma-related causes of anxiety and reduce the ones which affect you.

Each bout of anxiety gives your nervous system another opportunity to practice settling and relaxing. Over time, the parasympathetic nervous system becomes more active and you will return to a smooth rhythm of activation and settling.

Frozen! Thaw from Surrender

An overwhelming threat with no possibility of overcoming it results in a freeze response. See "Figure 1: Nervous System Activation Over Time" on page 116 (top of figure).

Mei Lin, who hates having her hands touched, tensed as the massage therapist worked down her arm. She wanted to ask the massage therapist to stop, but her throat closed around the words. She wanted to pull away, but could not move. She struggled silently with her discomfort until the massage therapist moved on to her neck, ashamed of her inability to speak up.

Protective surrender. A freeze response includes physical collapse, stillness, and dissociation from the body. As Peter Levine describes in *Waking the Tiger: Healing Trauma*,* a gazelle first flees a cheetah with all its strength, and then, when the cheetah is almost upon it, collapses to the ground in surrender. This shields the gazelle from pain when attacked, and could cause the cheetah to lose interest.

If the cheetah does wander off, the gazelle eventually trembles back into connection with itself. The trembling discharges the intense activation energy of the chase and allows the gazelle to settle back into peaceful grazing.

Interrupted activation cycle. In humans, social conditioning often interrupts the full activation cycle. Running from danger, yelling, fighting back, and trembling are politely

---

* Peter Levine, *Waking the Tiger: Healing Trauma*, North Atlantic Books, 1997.

suppressed, leaving activation energy trapped in the system. This decreases the system's capacity to handle stress and makes the freeze response more likely during the next threatening event. The trapped energy manifests as depression, general feelings of helplessness, and other signs of trauma.

Out of resources. We often view surrender as shameful, weak, or cowardly, even though a freeze response indicates that the nervous system and the body are out of resources.

We are tempted to judge because it was not a life-or-death situation, or because we could have taken a different action with more resources available. A recent freeze may also carry feelings of shame and terror stored from a past freeze in a more dangerous situation. We are taught to blame ourselves for not expressing our boundaries in words and actions, even though a frozen body is expressing urgent distress as best it can.

During a freeze. When you find yourself blocked from moving or speaking:

- Mentally name the freeze. "Oh, I'm frozen."
- Drop any "shoulds" about asserting boundaries.
- Breathe.
- Wait with kind awareness as the freeze continues and then thaws. You will thaw.

While you are frozen, these are the most constructive actions available whether you are in present danger or not. After you thaw, you can take action to address any danger.

Deep thaw. As you come out of a freeze in safety, you may feel exhausted and need rest. You may also come out feeling panicked, trapped, or helpless in a flashback to an earlier freeze experience. Remind yourself that **it ended** and you are alive and safe. Look around the room and ground yourself firmly in the present.

The panicked part of you may be outraged that you are (apparently) ignoring an emergency. Keep interrupting with, "It ended." Once the interruption takes hold, the panic subsides into slightly embarrassed relief that the emergency is finally over.

Tune in to your body. During the thaw, tune in to your body and allow any movements that arise. You may tremble, quiver, jerk, or gesture as old energy leaves your body. You may feel tingling or warmth as well.

As the reaction completes, alert calmness and engagement with the present return. Some people report seeing in color again, or noticing details of familiar environments for the first time.

Take action when you can. If certain situations trigger freezes for you, explore taking action before or after a freeze. When you protect yourself from situations that feel dangerous to your body, helplessness and disconnection are replaced with the direct experience of your strength and power in the present. As you heal, your perception of danger will change spontaneously. It is not necessary to push yourself through activities that feel threatening.

Mei Lin could tell massage therapists in advance that she does not want them to touch her hands. She can also ask them to check in with her if she becomes very still and to stop touching her if she does not respond. If a conversation in advance is still too difficult or triggering, Mei Lin can discontinue massage or change practitioners. It is neither therapeutic nor relaxing to receive bodywork while frozen.

Partial freeze. A freeze can involve the whole body, or

only a part. As Mei Lin moves through freezes with awareness, she notices that her voice and her hands are frozen, but she can still wiggle her toes and even push away with both feet.

Conflicting needs. Sometimes a freeze is the result of a double bind. Caught between the need to do something and the need not do it, the body locks up. For example, if someone witnesses abuse in the workplace but must ignore it to keep her job, the need to both turn toward it and turn away from it can lead to a chronically stiff neck.

If you feel deeply conflicted during a freeze, connect and ask your body what it wants to do, focusing on one need at a time. Simply bringing attention to each need can ease the conflict and restore movement.

Full permission to freeze. Freezing is a core physiological response we share with all mammals. When you give yourself full permission to feel helpless and frozen, it paradoxically creates space for healing and effective action.

Accept Suicidal Feelings

Suicidal thoughts and feelings are a rarely discussed after-effect of trauma. People often respond to suicidal disclosures with judgments and panic, even if there is no plan to carry out any suicidal actions. This article explores some of the many reasons for suicidal thoughts and feelings, offers some tools, and encourages acceptance rather than self-judgment when those thoughts and feelings arise.

If you do have a plan to carry out suicidal actions, please read "Thinking About Suicide? Read This First," online at www.metanoia.org/suicide/. Reach out for help! Call a suicide hotline such as 1-800-SUICIDE (1-800-784-2433), or your local emergency services at 911. You deserve help, and you deserve to live.

Clinical depression, biochemical imbalances, and Seasonal Affective Disorder (SAD) can cause suicidal thoughts and feelings, but are beyond the scope of this article. If you (or the people around you) suspect that you might be clinically depressed, please seek out professional assistance. In addition, the reasons and tools below may also apply to your situation.

Tell someone. Even without plans to act, it is helpful to break isolation and tell someone about how you feel. Whether you tell a therapist, clergy, doctor, or friend, choose your supporter carefully. Some people may be required to report your disclosure if you have a plan, and others may be emotionally unprepared to handle the conversation.

Wellspring of Compassion

Simply notice. If you are having suicidal thoughts or feelings, you may be responding with your own judgments and panic. Make room to simply notice the thoughts and the circumstances that surround them. Take a breath. Notice any sensations in your body.

Are there any patterns that emerge? Perhaps the thoughts come at around the same time of day, or around the same activities, or after interacting with the same people. Also observe what you do in response to the thoughts. Are some of your responses more soothing and helpful than others? Notice even your judgments and panic with gentle curiosity.

As you read the reasons for suicidal feelings and suggestions below, notice which ones resonate for you. Follow the ideas that carry a sense of hope and energy.

1. Chronic pain, illness, and exhaustion. Suicidal feelings can be a response to ongoing pain and discomfort, either emotional or physical, or both. If you have been hurting for a long time, you may be worn out, and suicidal feelings are a way of saying, "I need this to stop!"

Listen for inner demands. If you feel exhausted and overwhelmed to the point of suicidal feelings, make it a priority to get help. You deserve it! As much as you can, be a receptive listener to yourself, and also look for others who can listen to your feelings. Take those inner demands seriously, whether for more time for rest, a change in diet, stronger pain medication, more emotional support, or permission to cry.

2. Code for shame. Have you ever said, "I was so ashamed I wanted to die"? Sometimes, the thought, "I want to die!" is code for, "I'm feeling ashamed!" When shame is attached to the self ("I'm a bad person") rather than to behavior ("I did something bad"), it can be unbearably painful. The shame

ॐ 124 ॐ

is buried by unconsciously translating it into the thought about wanting to die.

Try a new sentence. Test this out by saying to yourself, "I'm feeling ashamed!" after you hear yourself thinking, "I want to die!" Does the new sentence ring solid and true, or does it seem hollow and false? If it rings true, try to remember what you were thinking and doing just before the suicidal thought arose and observe what might be triggering shame. With your kind attention, the shame may lighten and dissipate. If the shame feels overwhelming, focus on your breath and on the environment around you. Remember that no matter what you have done or experienced, your core self always deserves love and gentle care.

3. Reliving trauma. Suicidal feelings can be left over from a trauma where death seemed imminent, triggering a freeze. When defenses are overwhelmed, the body shuts down in shock and is not present to realize that it survived after all. In an attempt to complete the experience, the nervous system returns to the moment of trauma, and thoughts and images about death keep arising.

Gently and slowly work through the trauma. If you survived a car crash, surgery, assault, or other violent trauma, and you now experience recurring suicidal thoughts or images, you may need to gently and slowly work through the trauma to reawaken and integrate the parts that shut down.

It is difficult to shift your perspective on a near-death event by yourself. Reach out to someone who can help you work slowly to avoid retraumatization, widen trauma-narrowed perspective, and replace isolation with connection and support.

4. Threatened for telling. During childhood abuse, perpetrators sometimes implicitly or explicitly threaten the child with death if she or he tells anyone about the abuse. This can lead to suicidal thoughts or feelings in response to remembering and telling about the abuse.

Connect with your child self. If you feel suicidal just after disclosing, or even thinking about disclosing, some aspect of past abuse, you may be responding to old threats. Gently explain to your frightened child self that the abuser can no longer carry out the threat. Allow your child self to express and release fear by drawing pictures, writing in a journal (perhaps with your non-dominant hand), or wrapping up in a blanket.

Consider making an internal commitment to honor the fear and disclose the abuse only where and when it feels safe. The fear may be based on the past, and it may also be a subconscious response to unsafe aspects of your present situation.

Safety and acceptance. The first priority with suicidal thoughts and feelings is to stay safe. Once you separate the feelings from any possible actions, approaching the feelings with acceptance helps you connect with your self and resolve the feelings themselves.

Resources

Dr. Bessel van der Kolk, Founder and Medical Director of the Trauma Center in Boston, describes some of the physical changes in brain function and hormonal activity during trauma responses in his article "Clinical Implications of Neuroscience Research in PTSD."
www.traumacenter.org/products/pdf_files/NYASF.pdf

Dr. John Briere explains his self-trauma model in an academic article, "Treating adult survivors of severe childhood abuse and neglect: Further development of an integrative model."
www.johnbriere.com/STM.pdf

Jeannie Riseman explains the BASK (Behavior, Affect, Sensations, Knowledge) model of flashbacks in a short article, "BASK Flashbacks."
www.survivorship.org/resources/articles/psychology.html
(second article, scroll down)

Waking the Tiger: Healing Trauma, North Atlantic Books, 1997, by Peter Levine, contains groundbreaking information about the body's response to trauma and how to heal. Use caution: it also contains disbelief in response to a ritual abuse survivor's memories.

In an Unspoken Voice: How the Body Releases Trauma and Restores Goodness, Peter Levine, North Atlantic Books, 2010, contains a history and detailed description of Somatic Experiencing, his method for healing trauma.

The websites for Metanoia (metanoia.org) and Suicide Hotlines (suicidehotlines.com) contain a wealth of information about managing suicidal feelings.

6: Heal Your Boundaries

Trauma causes ruptures in personal boundaries through physical injury, emotional violation, and loss of a sense of control over one's life. Healing from trauma includes restoration of flexible, strong boundaries.

Our boundaries heal when we bring awareness to our internal preferences and limits, and allow that awareness to guide our choices. Breathing deeply into the private territory of our bodies helps us reconnect with our physical boundaries.

Anger arises reflexively when our boundaries are crossed, warning us to pay attention and consider taking action. We often confuse enforcement of boundaries with the boundaries themselves. Expressing our boundaries is an act of courage, since it makes our inner preferences more visible to the outside world.

While clear boundaries help respectful people treat us better, we will still encounter challenges at times. We can choose to distance ourselves from people who push our boundaries repeatedly, rather than believing that our boundaries are at fault.

As our boundaries heal, we learn to distinguish between

our own emotions and opinions and ones we have picked up from others. Sensitive people are especially prone to resonating with external emotions. Rather than striving to become impervious to other people's energy, the goal is to notice and release what does not belong to us. We also learn to care for our own inner children and let other people care for theirs.

We often make decisions based on "What will They think?" rather than looking inside for what is true for us. We think of Them as being external to us, but we carry Them as a committee inside. We can hire and fire committee members to better support our preferences and choices.

How do you currently relate to your boundaries? What emotions come up when you think about them?

Say Yes to Your Boundaries

"Name the action, criticize it, and tell them what to do with it." The self-defense instructor makes this three-step model sound easy. "Your hand is on my shoulder. I don't like it. Take it off." Her voice is calm, matter-of-fact. One by one we practice around the circle, receiving our neighbor's hand on our shoulder and calmly telling her to take it off.

Build skills. Before we can apply the three-step model in real situations, we need to build new skills:

- Trust our perceptions enough to name people's actions out loud.
- Connect with our boundaries so we know when an action violates them.
- Confidently claim our space.

Frequently noticing our sensations, emotions, and preferences builds all three skills.

We often think of boundaries as fences we must set up and patrol. We try to figure out the best place to put the fence based on how other people might react. If someone crosses the fence, or if surprise and fear keep us from immediately pushing them back, we perceive it as a boundary failure. Any hesitation in defending even the most obvious boundary allows the offender to blame the victim for being unclear.

Flexible container. Boundaries are already part of us, a flexible container for sensations, emotions, and preferences, separating "me" from "not-me". Instead of trying to create boundaries with our thoughts, we can discover and nourish the boundaries we already have.

Just as our skin marks the edges of our physical body, our boundaries mark the edges of our selves. Just as our skin heals from injuries, our boundaries heal from injuries caused by trauma and emotional abuse.

Define "too close." Next time you are in a crowd, observe your reaction when someone gets too close. You may notice: tight belly, clenched jaw, braced shoulders, a sinking feeling, anger, an impulse to move away, or sudden spaciness or distraction. What are your personal signs that someone is too close to you?

Also observe your reaction when someone is a comfortable distance from you. You may notice: relaxed breathing, open chest, warmth, ease. What are your personal signs that you have the space you prefer?

Note that "too close" is defined by your internal reactions in the moment, not by anyone's thoughts or opinions.

Listen for your answers. To nourish your boundaries, bring your attention to your sensations, emotions, and preferences. At least once a day, pause and ask yourself:

- What you notice
- How you feel
- What you want

Listen for your answers with room to be impractical, implausible, and unreasonable.

In the past, you may have been punished for expressing your feelings and wants. You may have found it too painful to articulate your wants even to yourself if you could not achieve them. You may worry about what other people think. You may have learned to dissociate to protect yourself. Gently acknowledge your reasons for pushing your perceptions and preferences away.

Can you become curious about your feelings and wants the way you are curious about a new friend? Your answers mark the edges of your being.

Choose what pleases you. As you learn about your preferences, keep an eye out for easy ways to move toward them. When there are no obstacles, you will naturally choose what pleases you. Notice how your body responds to those choices.

With more practice, you will be able to speak up for your preferences even in the face of obstacles. It can be scary to speak up. Other people may have their own agendas, and resist yours. At the same time, relief, delight, and even euphoria reward you when you say yes to your boundaries.

Rehearse for confrontations. Even after you become familiar with your boundaries and stand up for your preferences with other people, you may still need a short, clear way of telling someone they have crossed your line. Practice calmly applying the three step model in your imagination, or with your cat. "You nipped me. It hurts. Don't do that."

Even if you rarely use the three-step model out loud, it helps you clarify your boundaries for yourself.

Say yes to yourself. Every time you listen for what you notice, how you feel, and what you want, you are strengthening your connection with your boundaries and helping them heal. You're worth it!

Claim Your Space, Breathe into Your Back

Take a few moments to notice your breathing. What parts of your body move with your breath? Did your breathing change as you observed it? Do you hear any internal judgments about your breathing?

Your personal cathedral. Shallow chest breathing takes up as little space as possible. Deeper belly breathing pushes out into the world. Back breathing claims the space that is already yours, the three-dimensional cathedral arch of ribs, spine, and sternum waiting

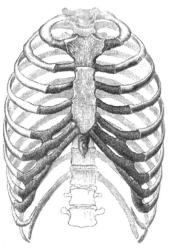

**Figure 2:
Human Rib Cage**[*]

to be filled and emptied and filled again by your breath.

Next time you are near a baby or a cat, watch her back expand as she breathes. We all breathed that way at first if we had freedom of movement, before we learned to suppress tears and shouts by holding our breath, before we learned to hold still instead of moving, before we started using our diaphragm as a storage closet instead of a breathing muscle.

Back breathing for singing. At a singing workshop this summer, I asked for help with breathing for singing.

[*] Image source and more information about the human rib cage: en.wikipedia.org/wiki/Human_rib_cage

The teacher placed her hands about half-way between my waist and armpits, thumbs around to my back, and asked me to push her thumbs away by breathing into them. At first I pushed into my shoulders, but then I found a way to breathe into the middle of my back.

It felt like my first full breath in thirty years. Joyful, effortless, once I remembered how. I could sing four times longer on a breath than I could before.

Try it for yourself. Put your hands on your waist, thumbs to the back, and then move your hands as far up and back as you comfortably can. Let the bones of your thumbs connect with the bones of your ribs with light pressure. As your breath flows in, allow those back rib bones to push your thumbs apart.

Experiment. You may struggle at first, pouring in more effort than you need. You may find your way, then lose it again. Keep playing with it.

How does it feel to breathe easily into your back? You may feel your torso filling like a barrel, expanding slightly all the way around. You may feel your lungs separating as they expand, like wings.

Think of a song you know, any song. Go back to the ABCs or Twinkle Twinkle Little Star if you have to. Sing it playfully, as if you were singing with your favorite four-year-old. Allow a full easy breath into your mid-back. How far do you get into your song before wanting to breathe again?

Now you can practice in the car or anytime you have privacy and a little spare time, singing to feel how much air you allowed to flow in.

Come home to your breath. When you notice dissociation, obsessive thoughts, or anxiety, use them as a reminder to practice back breathing. First acknowledge the pattern you noticed ("Ah, there it is") and then allow your mid-back to open to your breath. The shift in attention can lighten the pattern over time with the same effortlessness that fills your torso with air.

When you work with anger or boundaries, breathing into your back gives you space to notice what is true for you. Outside your body, you have to take other truths into consideration, but your inner territory belongs only to you.

Drop the effort. When we do not succeed at something, we often push harder and work longer. All the work in back breathing is in remembering how to stop working. Are there other areas in your life where less effort could lead to more ease and success?

Who Owns That Anger?

Anger is often labeled as a negative emotion, and many of us push it away or judge ourselves for not being "enlightened enough" when we feel angry. While anger does damage when held in or unleashed on another, it leads to clarity and strength when handled with care.

The key is to pause before acting, taking time to connect with the emotion and inquire into the reasons behind it. Here are three different reasons for anger and some positive ways to handle it.

1. Present boundaries. Anger is an instinctive, healthy response when someone crosses a boundary. It can be a surprise if the boundary was not conscious, or if the person acted so sweetly that the answering anger seems unreasonable.

For example, 27-year-old Zachary has been visiting his parents for several days. He comes in one day to find his dirty laundry washed and neatly folded. He knows his mother Corinna acted with love, and at the same time he notices the tightness in belly and jaw that signal anger for him.

Request a change. When he pauses to attend to his feelings, he realizes that the anger arose because she went through his belongings without asking. Zachary can now approach his mother kindly, thank her for doing his laundry, and also request that she honor his boundary around permission to touch his belongings.

Ideally, Corinna will blink, realize her son has grown up,

and acknowledge the boundary. No matter what her response, Zachary's ownership of his anger has alerted him to his boundary and allowed him to communicate with clarity and compassion.

2. Past triggers. At times, we do not have the resources or safety to process anger in the moment, so it is stored away in the body. Many days or even years later, a reminder can trigger the stored anger.

Perhaps Zachary recently broke up with his boyfriend, who often did the laundry for both men. This time, when Zachary takes a break to inquire into his anger at seeing his folded laundry, he connects with a blaze of unresolved grief and anger from the relationship.

Once a trigger is identified, it can be healing to avoid it in the short-term. Zachary could let Corinna know that he needs to do his own laundry for a while.

Release the emotions. Eventually, stored emotions do need to be released. It does not need to happen all at once. When time and privacy allow, we can sit with the emotions as they run their course, noticing the accompanying thoughts, sensations, and impulses. Writing in a journal, crying, and gentle movement can help. Reaching out for support can also help.

This could be an opening for Zachary to share some of his feelings about his breakup with Corinna. Owning his triggers allows Zachary to care for himself and his emotions without blaming others for accidentally reminding him of the past.

3. Contagious emotions. Although emotions seem private and internal, they can be contagious. Through subtle non-verbal communication, we sometimes find ourselves carrying emotions that belong to someone else.

Zachary returns to visit his parents a year later. His emotions around the past relationship have healed, and he brings his laundry to Corinna as they agreed. However, when he receives the clean laundry, he still notices tightness in his belly and jaw.

"What if..." He pauses to examine his reactions, but inquiring into present boundaries and past triggers leaves the discomfort unchanged. When he asks himself, "What if this anger isn't mine?" he feels immediate relief as the tightness eases.

Perhaps Corinna is feeling anger that she cannot yet acknowledge, and the laundry transaction non-verbally carried that anger to Zachary. Whether he chooses to mention his response to Corinna or not, Zachary is already freed from the anger by realizing that it is not his.

Anger is energy. When managed responsibly, anger is both a crucial signal that something is amiss and a source of power for change. Honoring and inquiring into anger supports strong, clear boundaries and healthy interactions with others.

Just-Right Visibility

"Mama, look at me!" Around the world, children demand to be seen, acknowledged, and celebrated as they express their authentic selves. Over time, they internalize their parents' warm regard and become their own compassionate witnesses. They continue to reach out to external witnesses as well.

Safety: looking inward and outward. With healthy socialization, children learn to look inward for their own impulses, and outward to see how their actions will affect others. "Yes, you want this toy. You can choose that other toy or wait until Stefan is done with this one." Both their impulses and others' needs are affirmed.

Fear: looking only outward. In abusive environments, children learn concealment and fear instead. They soon learn to focus entirely on their surroundings and do what is safe and approved. Their internal impulses are a source of shame rather than affirmation. "Is it bad to want this toy?" An Inner Critic develops to help the child discover and obey the rules.

Around the world, children run to their parents crying, except when their parents are causing their pain. Under the weight of family secrets, children learn to hide their pain, carefully observing how unhurt children act.

Take a moment to inquire what visibility means to you. What happens when you consider allowing your authentic self to be visible? Breathe into your back as you sit with any emotions, images, words, and sensations that arise.

Visibility means vulnerability, ridicule, injury, and blame.

Perhaps you have a story that always comes to mind, the time you tripped on stage in third grade, or the time you asked for a raise and the boss laughed. Breathe into that story with kindness. Allow it to be present, along with the cringing, shamed self who carries it.

Acknowledge your skills at hiding and avoiding visibility. Honor the choices you have made to guard yourself from exposure. Do you hold yourself erect to conceal your pain? Do you duck away from the limelight at work? Do you make small talk with people, or avoid talking to them at all? Breathe gently into all the ways you know how to hide.

Visibility means affirmation, sympathy, succor, and credit.

Perhaps you have another story about the time you taught a class and left the students joyfully alight with understanding, or the time you confided in your friend and she responded with quiet, perfect sympathy. Breathe into that story with kindness. Allow it to be present, along with the poised, confident self who carries it.

Acknowledge your skills at stepping forward and taking risks. Honor the choices you have made to allow your authentic self to shine forth. Do you sometimes allow yourself to flinch? Do you take on the new project and figure it out one step at a time? Do you create sculpture or music or writing or movement and allow someone else to witness your creation? Breathe gently into all the ways you know how to shine.

Visible boundaries. When you look inward as well as

outward, you notice your boundaries more easily. When you are willing to be visible to others, you can express your boundaries and ask others to honor them. When you only look outward in an effort to blend in with everyone else, your boundaries remain invisible to you and others.

Think back to environments where you had to conceal your boundaries. What helped you decide that was the safest action? What are the signs of an environment safe enough to make your boundaries visible? Observe what you feel in your body as you imagine one, and then the other.

Allow complexity. Check in again with your reactions to allowing your authentic self to be visible. Notice what happens when you breathe into your back and give yourself plenty of room to have many different reactions at once.

Visible to yourself. A big part of healing is willingness to be visible to yourself. Rather than a journey to somewhere else, healing is a discovery of what is already here. Moment by moment, you will decide how much visibility is just right for you.

Inner Child Lost -n- Found

Adults and their inner children get separated surprisingly often, sometimes through trauma, and sometimes simply through society's expectations of adults. The separation can cause intractable distress until the underlying problem is resolved.

If you find yourself saying "I've tried everything!" or "Don't leave me!" or "See me!" on a regular basis, visit the Inner Child Lost -n- Found for relief.

"I've tried everything!" You are a capable, self-aware adult, and you use a lot of great tools to manage your life. However, there is one problem area or pattern that you just cannot seem to fix. No matter how hard you try, you cannot find a way to feel better. You are exhausted, and you want a solution *now*.

Found: An imprint of someone else's inner child, energy, or emotions. Mirror neurons in our brains echo the expressions and body language of the people around us, recreating their emotions in our bodies. Our nervous systems automatically align with nearby nervous systems. This effect is strongest in infants and children and occurs in adults as well, especially sensitive ones.

For example, if your mother was often anxious, you may struggle with unquenchable anxiety.

Release the energy. Nothing you try is working because the problem is not yours to solve. Just considering the possibility that the problem is not yours can bring instant relief.

Visualize the external energy floating away from you and returning to its true home. You will find that all those great tools will suddenly work much better now that you are applying them to your own energy instead of someone else's.

"Don't leave me!" You know all about the dangers of codependence and you are doing everything you can to stand on your own two feet, and yet it is agonizing when your partner (or friend) wants some space. Even if the relationship is abusive, it feels like a catastrophe to envision separation.

Lost: Your own inner child. It sounds like you gave your inner child to someone else to raise. Perhaps your parents lacked the skills and resources to give you what you needed, and you are looking to your adult relationships to finish the job. This makes you as vulnerable and dependent as a child again. Fortunately, as an adult you have more options.

Raising inner children is an inside job. You can reach out to others for positive examples, support, and nurturing, and then bring those resources inside to help you tend your own inner child. You may need to grieve the parenting you did not receive before it feels possible to take over the job yourself. Beneath the grief and pain, you will find strength and independence as you learn the skills you need.

"See me!" You feel painfully lonely, even when you have people around you. You desperately want to be seen and accepted, and at the same time you need to appear strong and functional.

Lost: Compassion for your inner child. It sounds like you do your best to care for your inner child, and at the same time you find it hard to accept some of her or his qualities, such as vulnerability, weakness, or naiveté. Perhaps you endured abuse, and you hate that you were powerless to avoid it. It feels safer to believe that your young self could have done something different to control the outcome.

Sit with the feelings. It makes sense that you avoid the discomfort of vulnerability or other young feelings. It also makes sense that your inner child is lonely and desperate to be seen.

The conflict can be resolved by sitting with all your feelings for a few minutes at a time. You do not have to fix or change anything; just notice the feelings that arise. Your inner child will receive some of the attention he or she craves, and the short time limit ensures that you will not be overwhelmed. You will gradually get to know each other and come to live together more peacefully.

When you find yourself in extreme distress, or grappling with an issue that just will not get better, remember to visit the Inner Child Lost -n- Found for help. As you release energy that does not belong to you and reconnect with your own inner child, you will find calmness replaces the ongoing distress in your life.

Haunted by Shame? Change Your Committee

Boundaries separate what you think from what other people think, but it is not always easy to tell the difference.

"How could I have said that?!" With a hot blush, clenched stomach, wish to disappear, or inner scolding, we all come to recognize our responses to feeling shame. Unlike guilt, which is a negative judgment about an action and is open to amends, shame is a negative judgment about the self and feels permanent.

Shame is learned. As infants and small children, we expressed ourselves freely without worrying about what others thought. As we received negative responses from others, we learned to filter our behavior to be more acceptable in their eyes.

If we received abuse, we also absorbed the deeper shame of being victimized. Sadly, the shame that belongs to the abuser is often carried by the survivor, who tries ever more desperately to deserve the respectful treatment which is already everyone's birthright.

Trying to be good. To help us guess what would win the approval of the people around us, we internalize their judging voices to form a governing committee. The committee could be drawn from parents, teachers, community leaders, religious leaders, siblings, schoolmates, co-workers, TV personalities, and random encounters, like the guy who sneered as you walked by three years ago.

Many life choices, from tiny details ("What shall I wear today?") to major turning points ("How shall I make a living?") are influenced by what They think. It may feel like They are huge, amorphous, and outside you, but in reality They are your internal committee, available to you for observation and gradual change.

1. Who is on your committee? The first step is to narrow down "They" to specific voices. Whose opinion, specifically, are you worried about?

Choose a recent small decision — what to wear today, or what to eat for breakfast, for example — and notice what guided your final choice. Aside from the practicality of what is available, and the ease of habit, are there also guiding "shoulds"? Imagine making a radically unusual choice, for example your favorite party dress to go for a walk, or candy for breakfast. When you imagine reactions to your choices, who is reacting? Who says it is not allowed? Does anyone cheer you on? Make a list.

Now that you have a clearer idea of the committee membership, proceed with hiring and firing decisions.

2. Hire supporters. Ideally, your internal committee encourages and supports you in listening to your heart and making choices that work best for you. You may already have some supportive committee members, or this may be your first supportive hire.

Reflect on people who have played a supportive role in your life. Whether they are in your past or present, whether you know them personally or not, whether they are fictional or real, write down their names. If you cannot think of someone who consistently fills that role, think of supportive encounters you have had. If nothing comes to mind, imagine the supportive response you want to hear. "If it would bring you joy, I think it's a great idea to wear your party dress on a walk."

Now hire a supportive person (even if imaginary) for your internal committee. Make the support visible. Think of quotes that make you smile, and put them up where you will see them often. Add a picture if you have one. Imagine asking your supporter for feedback on your decisions and bask in the warmth and encouragement you receive.

Seek external support. Now that you brought attention to receiving internal support, seek out external support as well. Write down any compliments or positive feedback you receive. Just as you would choose a supporter when disclosing pain, notice how your body responds to people in your life, and spend more time with the ones who make you feel most comfortable.

3. Fire harsh critics. The critical voices on your internal committee are speaking from the past, not the present. If they cannot bring themselves up to date and begin supporting you, they need to be removed from their positions of power.

Choose a voice that seems least relevant to your life now. The person may have had power over you long ago, like a second grade teacher, or made one cruel remark that had a lasting effect, or is enforcing standards that you no longer agree with. Fire that voice!

To make your decision stick, first tell a story where their opinion matters, and then tell a new story where their opinion does not matter at all. Since this is all happening in the privacy of your mind, you get to choose which story to believe.

For example, first story: "That guy sneered at me because I look terrible." Second story: "That guy sneered because he was thinking about a bad TV show."

Firing critical voices can bring instant relief. If you still hear their negative messages, remind them that they were fired. You can also ask your supportive hires for corresponding positive messages.

Avoid external harshness. Are you receiving judgment or cruelty in the present? Notice any incidents that occur, and take action to minimize contact with people who treat you or others badly. Counteract their messages by listening to your supportive hires, and by reading your list of recent compliments.

Keep working on the hard cases. Some negative voices may take longer to remove. The former boss you have been trying to please for twenty years or the mother who taught you to diet because your body looks like hers will probably not respond to a single decision to fire them.

Keep hiring and listening to supportive voices. Keep rewriting those stories about the harsh voices until you deeply realize that their voices are not relevant today. Even your mother was thinking of herself and not you when she criticized you.

The places you'll go! Imagine living your life with a fully supportive, encouraging, and approving internal committee. The possibilities are limitless! If you hear grumpy voices saying that this cannot apply to you, thank them for their input, remind them that times have changed, and turn your attention to the supportive voices instead. What will you try first with their enthusiastic support?

Resources

Better Boundaries: Owning and Treasuring Your Life, New Harbinger Publications, 1997, by Jan Black and Greg Enns, explains why boundaries are important, and supports your boundaries with stories, tips, and exercises.

The Dance of Anger, Harper Paperbacks, 2005, by Harriet Lerner, contains advice for handling anger with care.

In *There Is Nothing Wrong With You: Going Beyond Self-Hate*, Keep It Simple Books, 2001, Cheri Huber explores how to look inside with kindness and allow your authentic self to come forth.

Robyn Posin's website <u>ForTheLittleOnesInside.com</u> passionately advocates for caring for our own inner children. "Others' Views" recounts her painful learning process in an enmeshed relationship.
<u>www.forthelittleonesinside.com/mpage/othrsvus.html</u>

Finding Your Own North Star: Claiming the Life You Were Meant to Live, Three Rivers Press, 2002, by Martha Beck, is funny, honest, and full of tools to heal and grow. Her section about changing your "Everybody" inspired the article about changing your committee.

7: Learn to Thrive

As we continue to connect with ourselves, work through trauma reactions, and heal our boundaries, we bring our attention to thriving in the present.

Some of the energy that went toward surviving can now flow into creativity. We can make choices that suit us in all aspects of our lives, including holiday traditions and maintaining our homes.

Trauma survivors, like everyone, struggle with relating to others and have certain difficult patterns that keep reappearing in our lives.

Over time, our compassion flows with fewer obstructions, and we treat ourselves with more consistent kindness and forgiveness, giving ourselves room to thrive. Take some time to celebrate your life skills and the ways you are already thriving.

Create: Walk into Fog

Whatever you can do or dream you can, begin it.
Boldness has genius, power and magic in it.
— W.H. Murray (often misattributed to Goethe*)

Unlike the healing process, which I experience as growing like a tree, I experience the creative process as a journey, exploring an unknown landscape obscured by fog. The created work rarely matches the initial vision, since an essential part of creativity is the commitment to walk into the unknown.

A common saying in twelve-step groups is "Don't compare your insides to someone else's outsides." Similarly, don't compare your creative work-in-progress to someone else's completed work. A thousand invisible decisions lie behind any completed project, including the repeated decision, moment by moment, to keep moving forward.

Not creative? Maybe you think you are not creative because you never learned how to draw or your childhood efforts met with criticism. Maybe trauma has forced you to focus on survival, and creativity seems like a distant luxury. Maybe it does not feel safe to commit to a process you cannot fully control.

One decision. When creating something new, like walking into dense fog, you can only see far enough to make one decision at a time. Each decision requires exploration and

---

* "German Myth 12: The Famous 'Goethe' Quotation."
http://german.about.com/library/blgermyth12.htm

possibly some false starts. When you do take a step forward the fog swirls and shifts, allowing you to see a new section of landscape to make the next decision.

Stories about other people's creative processes can give you a rough map of the territory and help you focus on the next decision to explore. Seek out guides and supporters who encourage you to trust your own creative voice.

Creating articles. I have walked into the unknown every month for three years writing these articles. Once, memorably, the topic, title, structure, and content flowed easily, and I found a perfect matching photograph two weeks early.

Usually, I struggle with one or more choices up to the day I send out the article. Back in English class, I was taught to create a structure and then start writing. In practice, a structure emerges halfway through the process, or I am rearranging paragraphs at the last minute. I changed the guiding metaphor of one nearly-completed article three times, finally returning to the one I started with.

Fear and anxiety. Each month, I wrestle with fear that the article will not come together, as well as anxiety about making my internal landscape visible. When my Inner Critic highlights boulders and roadblocks, I negotiate around them by giving myself permission to write a shorter, more personal, or more playful article than I originally intended. Once, she blocked the way so adamantly I changed course by including her voice. Her critical eye does help polish the articles at the end of the process.

Focused contemplation. I have learned to focus on a topic early in the month, giving me time to gather thoughts and experiences about it. I often notice related conversations in client sessions throughout the month. As W.H. Murray noted, beginning and commitment have their own magic

When I worry about finding a topic, my attention is on the fog itself, which remains impenetrable. When I say instead, "I wonder what topic I could write about," soon enough ideas float up and I can choose one that feels open to development. Similarly, I receive answers to focused contemplation about "I wonder how I can structure this," or "What would make a good example?"

Set time aside. Each article takes two days of solid work, so I look ahead in my schedule and set time aside to write. When the time arrives, it can be hard to find an initial foothold in the fog. Sometimes I start with an old-fashioned notebook and pen, especially on enticing sunny days when I want to write outside. Sometimes ideas flow during a break for a bike ride or washing dishes. Sometimes I circle around with related tasks on the computer before finally settling in to write.

Accidental exposure to gluten or fragrances leaves me unable to focus for days no matter what I do. When that happens, I have learned to simply accept the delay and reschedule.

Turning point. Once I start writing, the path through the fog is different every time. In some cases, it is a challenge to narrow the topic to article length, and in other cases I am surprised by what emerges when I need a few more sentences. Sometimes I find myself writing part of a different article before returning to the one I am working on, and once the new topic took over entirely.

Pushing through doubt to find the next foothold, adding ideas and making decisions, I reach a turning point where a new article is visible through the fog and I can complete it with confidence. I feel relieved and proud of its unexpected shape every time.

You are creating. Do you have a creative work-in-progress, or one you would like to begin? Sit with that question and allow ideas to bubble up.

What decision can you focus on next for your project? Listen for an answer as the possibilities sift through the back of your mind. Take notes. Ask again just before bed, first thing in the morning, or at the beginning of a walk. What supports your creative voice? What interferes with it?

Even if you are creating nothing else, your life itself is a creative project. One decision at a time, you are making your way across an unknown foggy landscape. As you make friends with both your internal source of ideas and your ways of handling uncertainty, you can find relief and pride in each step you take.

Choose Your Traditions

Traditional holidays can be a difficult time for trauma survivors, whether the trauma was a divorce, car accident, or childhood abuse. In the US, on top of the stresses of winter weather, short days, and taking time for holiday preparations, there is an added pressure and expectation to be happy. "Merry Christmas!" everyone says, without wondering whether the recipient is merry, or even Christian. "Have a Happy Thanksgiving," can be a hard sentence to hear if there is no family feast planned.

The following steps can ease some of the pressure around the holidays and help you create celebrations you enjoy.

Notice your expectations. Most of us have an internal script for how a holiday "should" go, acquired from our childhood experiences, stories we heard, and advertising. To make this script more explicit, choose a holiday and imagine a picture-perfect celebration:

- Who is there with you?
- What are those relationships like?
- What food does everyone eat?
- What is given?
- What is received?
- What are the sounds and sights and smells?
- How do you feel during the celebration? After?
- What else is important about the event?

Take notes or write a story or draw a picture of how the

holiday should be.

Honor your feelings. When you have some time and privacy, sit with your script and observe what feelings come up. Perhaps you have some judgments about your expectations. Just notice that.

If your holidays are likely to be very different from what you imagined, you might feel longing, grief, and anger. Allow the feelings to flow, and write or speak any words that come. Maybe your reality is closer to your ideal than you thought, and you feel surprise and gratitude. Whatever mix of feelings arises, let them all move through you.

Notice your desires. When you were sitting with your feelings, did you notice any aspects of the picture-perfect celebration that did not sound appealing? Allow yourself to daydream about a holiday celebration that would be comfortable and delightful for you. You can make small changes to your script, or start from scratch and imagine something completely different.

Again, fill in the details, answering the same questions you answered for your expectations. Take notes or write a story or draw a picture of your ideal holiday.

Open the door to action. As you pay attention to your expectations, feelings, and desires, do any possible actions come to mind? Often, tuning in to that ongoing internal mutter of expectations and judgments can ease conflict and open the door to movement toward what we want. Notice any parts of your ideal holiday that you can bring to life this year, and give yourself permission to take action.

Do you always spend the holidays with your contentious extended family when you really want peace and quiet in front of your home fireplace? Maybe you can shorten the family time to make room for some peaceful time for yourself, or at least take a long walk on your own.

Do you spend the holidays alone and you really want some company? Maybe you can find a community event or "Orphans Thanksgiving" to join, or you can find a friend who also wants company, or share time on the phone with someone. Homeless shelters and food banks always appreciate holiday volunteers.

Do you miss a dish your grandmother always baked? Maybe you can research the recipe through your family, or online, and make it for yourself.

Do you crave rest? How does it feel to imagine saying "No" to some of the tasks you associate with the holidays? Is there anything you can delegate or eliminate from your to-do list?

Are religious services part of your ideal holidays? Some religious communities offer special holiday services for people who are grieving or troubled, such as "Blue Christmas" or "Longest Night" services.

Did you experience twisted religious services as part of ritual abuse? Reach out for support and make self-care the highest priority during this triggering time of year. There will come a year when you can observe the triggers without being overwhelmed by them, separating the present from the past.

Listen lovingly to your heart. As much as you can, be gentle with yourself through the winter holidays. Create some space to feel however you feel, and honor your desires, however big or small they are, however possible or impossible they seem. Give yourself open permission to wish, and want, and daydream. Listen to your heart as you would to a small, trusting child.

The Joy of Maintenance

The day my controlling girlfriend moved out, I grabbed a broom and swept the wood floor with increasing relief and joy. She had subtly taken over my home by taking over the housework "as a favor." On that day, my view of maintenance tasks permanently changed from annoying interruptions to affirmations of presence. As I move through my space, I notice disorder and take pleasure in creating order.

Internal and external chaos. One sign of trauma is difficulty with self-care. Cleaning and other maintenance tasks seem both overwhelming and unimportant when confronting the pain of trauma.

At the same time, external chaos can make it more difficult to regain inner calm, subconsciously reinforcing feelings of worthlessness or helplessness. Reconnecting with your surroundings and making changes to match your preferences can create a positive cycle of external and internal order.

Pay attention peacefully. Look around your space, peacefully, without an agenda. Let your eyes wander, pausing when something catches your attention. What leaps out at you? Is there anything that has been there all along but you have not noticed in a while? Is there anything that makes you smile?

If you hear your Inner Critic or an echo of a parental voice presenting you with a list of chores left undone, acknowledge the voice and bring your attention back to the room around you.

Intention. Do you have an overall quality or intention for your home? Mine is "comfortable," and over the years, many people have spontaneously told me my home feels comfortable. What do people say about your home? Does it match your intended quality? How does your home feel to you?

Consider one change. Look around again. Allow your attention to rest on a single change you could make to your space to align it with your intention. It could be as small as putting a piece of paper in the recycle bin. If a big change comes to mind such as rearranging furniture, break it down into steps and think about the first step.

Does your body tighten and contract in response to the thought of that single change, or open and relax?

Inquire into tension. There are many possible reasons for your body to tighten against an action. Take some time to gently inquire. Which reasons resonate for you?

- The action might cause physical pain.
- You might encounter something that causes emotional pain.
- Someone might object.
- The change is a "should" rather than something you want.
- The action feels too big or overwhelming.

Make it easier. Now that you looked at some reasons for tightening, you could persist with this change, or start again with a different one. If you stay with this one, think about how to make it easier:

- You could move slowly and gently, or accomplish the action in a different way to avoid pain.
- You could decide in advance how to handle any

triggering or upsetting objects you come across, perhaps by putting them aside.

- You could negotiate with others about shared space, or claim some space of your own.
- You could change "should" to "could" and set your own priorities.
- You could break the action down further into smaller steps, or ask for help.

Experiment with action. Whether your body relaxed or tightened, does it feel right to take the action you are considering? If you do, is it easier, harder, or the same as you expected? If you do not, what is your experience of consciously choosing not to act?

Take another look around your space. What comes to your attention this time? You could repeat the experiment with a different change, or stop there.

Choices rather than chores. We often treat ourselves like a controlling parent around our chores. As you connect with yourself and your space, you can make more gentle choices about which maintenance tasks to do and which to set aside. Gradually, your home will align with your intention and become your haven.

Compassion for the Drama Triangle

Many of us struggle with difficult relationships at home, at work, or in our communities. The Drama Triangle model can help clarify an interpersonal situation when:

- You find that there is no right answer.
- People consistently misinterpret what you say.
- You feel that your role is pre-scripted.
- You notice a lot of shame and blame.
- The same words and scenes repeat often.

Dr. Stephen Karpman developed the Drama Triangle as a part of Transactional Analysis in 1968,* and it has been applied and adapted in many directions since then.

The Drama Triangle model has three interlocked roles:

- The **Victim** passively receives the actions of the Persecutor and Rescuer.
- The **Rescuer** defends and takes care of the Victim.
- The **Persecutor** attacks the Victim.

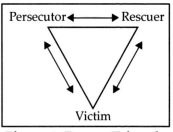

Figure 3: Drama Triangle

As the arrows in Figure 3 indicate, people can shift roles at any time. The perceived roles often depend on who is telling the story. One person can occupy all three roles in an internal conflict.

---

* Stephen Karpman, "Fairy Tales and Script Drama Analysis," 1968. www.karpmandramatriangle.com/pdf/DramaTriangle.pdf

Benefits. All three roles carry the benefit of maintaining an external focus instead of addressing internal pain, needs, and truths. The roles can be comfortably familiar even though the drama itself is uncomfortable. The Victim benefits by avoiding conflict and responsibility. The Rescuer feels needed, and the Persecutor feels powerful.

For example, Janine often comes home late from work. She casts herself as the Victim and her boss as the Persecutor. Her partner Antonia, as Rescuer, rearranges her schedule to compensate. Sometimes Antonia perceives herself as a Victim of Janine's inability to set boundaries with her boss. When she loses her patience, she yells at Janine about it, shifting into Persecutor. Janine may shift into Rescuer in response and agree to make changes, but her resentment continues to fuel the drama.

Exit the Drama Triangle. The key to interrupting a Drama Triangle is to witness it with compassion and curiosity.

A **witness** brings awareness. Observe how your body feels when you are embroiled in drama. When you feel frustrated or stuck about an interaction, ask yourself if a Drama Triangle might be operating, and who plays which roles.

Compassion knows that all of the participants are meeting their needs as best they can with the skills and resources available to them in the moment. Bring compassion to yourself most of all as you look at roles you have played and truths you have avoided.

Curiosity opens the door to honest self-examination as well as listening for other's truths. New information eventually ends the drama.

You can practice seeing the roles in past situations or even imaginary ones, since dramas tend to recur over and over.

Janine notices that she feels resentful and trapped after

her latest promise to set limits with her boss. She and Antonia have been repeating the same argument, a clear sign of a Drama Triangle. She takes a long solo walk, and kindly inquires into the struggle.

Focusing on the bigger picture rather than recent details, she honors both herself and Antonia for doing their best. With compassion, she perceives Antonia's "unwarranted attack" (Persecutor role) as part of her ongoing frustration with their schedules.

Janine also brings compassionate curiosity to her own avoidance of responsibility for her choices (Victim role). This job is important to her career, and she notices fear that Antonia will ridicule her priorities. With this new understanding, she returns home. Her internal shift will allow the couple to have a different conversation even if Antonia continues in a drama role.

Resistance to change. One person's honesty sometimes dissolves a conflict. Other times, bringing compassion and curiosity to an ongoing drama can be perceived as Persecution by participants who are unready for change. When a past Victim takes concrete action, or a past Rescuer says, "This is not my problem," or a past Persecutor makes genuine amends, they may receive intense pressure to continue their roles. It may take many small steps to disengage from a long-standing Drama Triangle.

Drama-free. With time and practice, you will recognize drama signs more quickly and spend less time entangled in the three roles. Celebrate each time you are more compassionate and honest with yourself and others, even if it does not lead to a swift harmonious resolution in every situation.

Not Again! Tame Your Fiercest Patterns

Not again! Despite your best efforts, your fiercest pattern has you in its claws. Your current relationship is turning out just like the last three, or your bank account is empty, or some other area of your life is in complete disarray.

In that moment of grim recognition, your Inner Critic piles on the shame and "shoulds," saying that everyone else has this figured out and you are obviously not trying hard enough. On top of the pattern itself, you feel desperation about your inability to fix it.

Hold still, move in. When my cat hooks my hand with her claws, I hold still and move my hand toward her to get unhooked. The same idea works with a recurring pattern.

Hold still by naming the experience you are having right now in its rawest form:

- "I am having the experience of not getting what I need."
- "I am having the experience of not being seen."
- "I am having the experience of my boundaries being violated."

What words convey your experience? Pause. Breathe. This is where you are right now.

You are not alone. We each have a unique set of strengths and tools to apply to our problems. Some problems yield so easily that we barely notice them, and we wonder why others do not manage them as well as we do. Some problems require a lot of hard work, but the progress is clear.

A few leftover problems are unaffected or even exacerbated by our particular strengths and tools. Those become our recurring patterns. We all have them.

Next time your Inner Critic tells you to try harder, remember that you are doing your best with the resources you have. Since your tools do not fix this problem, holding still and naming the experience could be your best option.

Move in. Now that you gained a sliver of relief by naming your experience, move in and unhook the claws by becoming a world expert in your pattern. Study it with interest. Consider keeping a lab notebook for your observations.

You experience this pattern a lot, and you already know a lot about it. You probably have a long list of attempts that have not worked. Honor your efforts! In science, negative results are just as important as positive results.

With kind curiosity, look at how the pattern has started and run its course in the past. As much as you can, skip over fault, or blame, or who was right and wrong. Simply look at what happened and how you responded.

Study the present as well, noticing your sensations and emotions when you are in the grip of the pattern. What happens in your body as part of this experience you named?

Notice the changes. Every time the pattern comes around, it can seem as if you are trapped in a loop which will never change. At the same time, you continue to acquire new information, skills, and awareness. You are on a spiral rather than a loop, moving through the pattern slightly differently each time. Take note of even the smallest differences. Think back a few years or ask a compassionate friend, and you may realize that the changes add up to big shifts.

Also remember that "never" and "forever" are flashback markers. Unprocessed traumatic memories can mysteriously draw similar events into your life in an effort to heal. As you hold still and move in toward the pattern, the traumatic memories have an opportunity to integrate into ordinary narrative memory.

Trust your senses. As an expert, you are sensitive to the merest hint of the pattern. Your Inner Critic may accuse you of projecting it into the world. Revisit that list of all the fixes you tried. Trust that you are not secretly trying to make yourself miserable. If you are sensing the pattern, there is a good reason.

Watch your pattern in action. As painful as it is to see a pattern coming and be unable to change it (this time), the act of observation is already a change. Pause. Breathe. Name your experience moment by moment, including the frustration and despair of being in the pattern again. Bring in as much gentleness and support as you can.

Hidden strengths. Recurring patterns highlight your weaknesses and at the same time show your hidden strengths. Is it easy for you to intuit and follow someone's wishes (even though you want clearer boundaries)? Is it easy for you to relax and not sweat the small stuff (even though you would prefer to know where your keys are)? You may not be getting the results you want, but there is still ease there. As you become an expert in your pattern, notice and celebrate your strengths.

Tame, not banish. We want to banish our fiercest patterns, but we have to learn to live with them instead. When we name and study our experiences, we get clawed less when patterns recur. As they become tamer, we may even come to grudgingly appreciate them.

Allow Self-Forgiveness

Self-forgiveness is entwined with sticky topics for survivors of abuse and trauma: forgiving others, acceptance, faith, and trust. To allow self-forgiveness, we gently question our layers of reflexive self-judgment.

One more task. Too often, people recommend forgiving others to sidestep appropriate rage and protect abusers from natural consequences of their behavior. "He's being nice now," they say, or, "She never bothers me." Forgiveness becomes a cruel yardstick for healing, one more task before survivors can feel good enough.

In contrast with the positive spin on forgiving others, self-forgiveness is sometimes framed as "letting yourself off the hook," as if self-judgment were the only way to improve. You can both forgive yourself for the past and resolve to change your behavior in the future. Self-forgiveness opens the door to change by releasing resistance and deepening your connection with yourself. Can you allow yourself to be imperfect and trust that you are doing your best?

Forgiveness for vulnerability. In some cases, self-forgiveness decreases forgiveness for others. In our efforts to protect and forgive abusers, we blame ourselves for "inviting" abuse. When we can forgive ourselves for being vulnerable, trusting, or simply finding ourselves in the vicinity of an abuser, we may feel less forgiving of the person choosing abusive behavior, at least for a while.

Extend kindness. In other cases, self-forgiveness works

in tandem with forgiveness for others. We are often most judgmental of qualities we cannot acknowledge in ourselves. When we can view our behavior with kindness, we can extend that kindness to others as well.

When we draw a line between acceptable and unacceptable people, we worry about staying on the correct side of the line. When we soften the line for others, we can relax that vigilance for ourselves.

Boundaries take priority. Some people define forgiveness as, "Let's pretend it never happened." Forgiveness does not eliminate grief, pain, and intolerance of abusive behavior. Boundaries take first priority, and it can be easier to forgive from a safe distance.

Forgiveness makes room for the way things are. Forgiveness is giving up all hope of having had a different past.* In addition, self-forgiveness is giving up all hope of being a different person.

Forgiveness is private and internal. It is a boundary violation to pressure anyone to forgive, including yourself. The shortest path to forgiveness is to give yourself ample room to experience all your unforgiving emotions.

Forgiveness happens in its own time, like a tense muscle letting go when all the reasons for tension are resolved. Muscle tension serves many purposes:

- Stabilize an injury
- Hold back emotions
- Tolerate pain
- Brace for impact
- Get through an emergency

---

* Martha Beck (slightly misquoting Lily Tomlin), *Leaving the Saints*, Three Rivers Press, 2006.

We can order muscles to relax, but it rarely works for long. When we resolve any present-day issues and connect with muscles to let them know that the emergency is over, they relax. The emotional tension of anger and old grudges relaxes into forgiveness in response to apologies, amends, and improved behavior, as well as time to grieve and heal.

Possibilities. How do you respond to the following ideas for self-forgiveness? Do you tighten up in refusal? Do you take a breath of relief? Do you hold still as you take in new possibilities?

Difference and sameness. You could forgive yourself for being the only strong, whole person in a family scarred by abuse and dysfunction. You could forgive yourself for being the only person falling apart in a family that appears serenely functional. You could forgive yourself for following in your family's footsteps.

Growth and change. You could forgive yourself for the wandering path that has led you to this moment. You could forgive yourself for learning things the hard way, for taking the easy way out, for being too young to know better, for being too old to begin, for trusting people who betrayed you, for betraying people who trusted you, for all your big and small decisions along the way.

Boundaries. You could forgive yourself for listening to your boundaries and saying no, or yes. Sometimes everyone involved is waiting uneasily for someone else to step forward, and your action is greeted with relief. You could forgive yourself for freezing and saying nothing at all.

You could forgive yourself for avoiding people who scare you. You could forgive yourself for staying close to people who repeatedly hurt you. It is easy to feel ashamed of kindness and love toward abusers. Instead, take pride in the kindness and love inside you.

Mistakes. You could forgive yourself for making mistakes, starting with tiny mistakes like leaving an unnecessary light on and continuing to catastrophic mistakes that caused ongoing harm. Are there any apologies and amends you want to make? Mistakes are part of being alive, part of not knowing the future or even everything about the present.

Injury and illness. You could forgive yourself for actions that led to a chronic injury. Back pain may start after lifting a heavy box, but the underlying cause is likely to be a complicated mix of one's physical and emotional history. You are doing your best to be healthy in each moment. Illness and pain are not a sign of failure, and even if they were, you could forgive yourself for them.

Your body. You could forgive your body for being too fat, too thin, too strong, too weak, too much of this and not enough of that and exactly the body it is right now. You could forgive your body for being sensitive to some things and insensitive to others. You could forgive your body for remembering trauma and reminding you with symptoms.

You could connect with your body and ask its forgiveness for disconnection. How do you feel as you listen for a response? Bodies are usually delighted to reconnect and do not hold grudges.

Already forgiving. As you consider the possibilities for self-forgiveness, acknowledge how much you have already forgiven yourself and others. No matter how much rage and turmoil you feel about some issues, there are many offenses you let pass with a shrug or worked through over years. Allow yourself to wonder: What would it be like to give up all hope of being a different person?

Resources

Bird by Bird: Some Instructions on Writing and Life, Anchor Books, 1995, is Anne Lamott's acerbic, funny, honest advice on handling the difficulties of being a writer.

The Joy Diet: 10 Daily Practices for a Happier Life, Crown Publishers, 2003, by Martha Beck, has helpful tips for creating a life that suits you, and has nothing to do with food.

FlyLady.net is a light-hearted, practical guide to remedying CHAOS ("Can't Have Anyone Over Soon") one baby-step at a time.

Stephen Karpman's original paper "Fairy Tales and Script Drama Analysis," 1968, and "The New Drama Triangles," 2007, provide more details and explanation of his drama triangle model and its applications.

www.karpmandramatriangle.com/pdf/DramaTriangle.pdf

www.karpmandramatriangle.com/pdf/
thenewdramatriangles.pdf

Taming Your Gremlin: A Surprisingly Simple Method for Getting Out of Your Own Way, Harper Paperbacks, 2003, by Rick Carson, emphasizes the themes of Simply Noticing and Playing with Options in a compact, playful format. Highly recommended.

Afterword: Wellspring of Compassion

Each article in this book touches on a different element of self-compassion and self-forgiveness as you heal from trauma. Take a moment to look inside with open attention. My hope is that you find compassion welling up and flowing to your body, your emotions, your brokenness, and your wholeness.

Celebrate any change or no change as the perfect outcome for you in this moment. Celebrate your survival, your tenacity, your perseverance, your exhausted surrenders and your joyous triumphs. Celebrate your presence in the world!

Does this book spark a response in you? I'd love to hear about it! Send your thoughts to sonia@TraumaHealed.com.

Glossary

Activation — Tension and increased stress, "fight, flight or freeze" response of the sympathetic nervous system. See also **Settling**. See "Anxiety, Your Relaxation Coach" on page 115.

Alter — A persona or internal voice. See also **Multiple personalities**.

Boundaries — A flexible container for sensations, emotions, and preferences, separating "me" from "not-me". See "Say Yes to Your Boundaries" on page 131.

Dissociation — Spaciness, disconnection, feeling distant from current experience. See "Gain Awareness of Dissociation" on page 38.

Dissociative Identity Disorder (DID) — A formal diagnosis for someone who has **multiple personalities.** Formerly known as Multiple Personality Disorder (MPD).

Double bind — A situation where any choice leads to punishment, you can't leave, and you can't discuss the situation. Used to display power and gain control over others. See "Step Away from Double Binds" on page 85.

Drama Triangle — Three interlocked roles of Victim,

Rescuer, and Persecutor. People involved in the drama can fluidly shift roles, or all three roles can be internal to one person. See "Compassion for the Drama Triangle" on page 162.

Emotional abuse — The use of words, body language, and other behaviors to bully someone into feeling defective. See "Emotional Abuse: You Deserve Better" on page 89.

Faith — Your deepest certainties and longings about your connection with Spirit. See "Spiritual Abuse: Take Back Your Faith" on page 96.

Flashback — Intrusive sensations, emotions, and reactions from the past which impinge on a trauma survivor's present-day life. Flashbacks are a hallmark symptom of **PTSD**. See also **Trigger**. See "Flashbacks: Experience Distress in Safety" on page 111.

Flashback hangover — A feeling of rawness and fragility for a few hours or days after experiencing a **flashback**.

Flashback markers — Words such as "never," "always," or "forever" that indicate an experience, thought, or emotion is frozen in time. See also **Flashback**.

Freeze — Physical collapse, stillness, and dissociation from the body in response to an overwhelming threat with no possibility of overcoming it. See "Frozen! Thaw from Surrender" on page 119.

Inner Critic — Internal voice that tells you everything you have done, are doing, and will do wrong. See "Calm Your Inner Critic" on page 48.

Inner Nurturer — Internal voice that knows you deserve care and respect and there is nothing wrong with you. See "100 Percent On Your Own Side" on page 25.

Internal committee — Your internal "They" as in, "What would They think if I took that job?" You can hire and fire committee members. See "Haunted by Shame? Change Your Committee" on page 146.

Meditation — Sit comfortably, take three slow breaths, and notice what happens. Okay, now do it again. And again. There, you're meditating! See "Meditation: Safe Space for Noticing" on page 56.

Multiple personalities — Containing two or more internal voices with defined, separate personas (**alters**). A survival strategy, usually in response to complex trauma at a young age. Formally diagnosed as **Dissociative Identity Disorder (DID)**. See "Many Voices, All Valid" on page 60.

Post-Traumatic Stress Disorder (PTSD) — A label for the nervous system's long-term response to trauma. Diagnostic symptoms include intrusive memories (**flashbacks**), avoidance and emotional numbing, and anxiety and increased emotional arousal. See "5: Understand Post-Traumatic Stress Disorder (PTSD)" on page 101.

Red flag — A small boundary violation which could be a warning sign for larger violations in the future. See ""Trust Me!" and Other Red Flags" on page 81.

Resource — A source of support and strength. Resources can be external, such as a friend or a safe place, or internal, such as taking a deep breath to connect with the present moment. See "Remember at Your Own Pace" on page 107.

Ritual abuse — Prolonged, extreme, sadistic abuse in a group setting. Any ideology can be used to control group members, break their spirits, and justify torture. See "Spiritual Abuse: Take Back Your Faith" on page 96.

Sensitivity — Awareness of and vulnerability to one's physical and emotional environment. See "Signs of Sensitivity" on page 7.

Self-care — Meeting yourself where you are right now with kind attention. See "Introduction: Welcome" on page 1.

Settling — Relaxation and decreased stress, "rest and digest" response of the parasympathetic nervous system. See also **Activation**. See "Anxiety, Your Relaxation Coach" on page 115.

Spiritual abuse — When any abuser damages the victim's sense of worth, purpose, or connection to Spirit, or when a spiritual official causes harm to a congregation member. See "Spiritual Abuse: Take Back Your Faith" on page 96.

Trauma — An event or ongoing situation which overwhelms a person's available coping skills. See "Signs of Trauma" on page 5.

Trigger — An internal or external experience that stimulates a traumatic memory. Triggers can come through any of the senses, or through a thought or emotion. They can be subtle, such as the light at a certain time of year. Trigger can also refer to a physical sensitivity, for example, "Chocolate is one of her migraine triggers." See "Flashbacks: Experience Distress in Safety" on page 111.

Victim-blaming — The belief that if victims had behaved differently, they would not be coping with bad news now, so it must be their fault. No one deserves abuse for any reason. See "Demand Respect, Not Victim-Blaming" on page 78.

About the Author

Sonia Connolly offers intuitive, compassionate bodywork in Portland, Oregon for sensitive people healing from trauma. She is a survivor of incest, emotional abuse, and ritual abuse, and has sensitivities to gluten and fragrances. She finds joy in helping people heal, meditation, creativity, bicycling for transportation, gardening, petting her cat, and Balkan dancing and singing.

Learn more and sign up for free healing articles at TraumaHealed.com.

CPSIA information can be obtained at www.ICGtesting.com
Printed in the USA
BVOW02s1856100816

458617BV00001B/14/P